DECEIVERS EVER

DECEIVERS EVER

Memoirs of a Camouflage Officer 1939-1945

Steven Sykes

SPELLMOUNT LTD
TUNBRIDGE WELLS, KENT

First published in the UK in 1990 by
Spellmount Ltd
12 Dene Way, Speldhurst
Tunbridge Wells, Kent TN3 0NX
ISBN 0-946771-54-5

Typesetting by Vitaset, Paddock Wood, Kent
Printed by the KPC Group, Ashford, Kent

CONTENTS

In the Spellmount/Nutshell Military list:

First cooked meal in 0880 Strongpoint D + 1

Major Steven Sykes

PROLOGUE

There's a long long trail a-winding
Into the land of my dreams,
Where the nightingales are singing
And a white moon beams.
There's a long long night of waiting
Until my dreams all come true;
Till the day when I'll be going down
That long long trail with you.

Stoddart King, 1829-1933

The singers – a company of khaki-clad Officers Training Corps boys; the time – a summer night in 1932; the place – the military training area near Tidworth Camp; the occasion – marching back to camp after night operations; the atmosphere – a strange, strong, almost nostalgic awareness of the Great War, and an even stronger foreboding of another great war to come.

It was 14 years since the First World War and seven years of uneasy peace until the second. As a child I had listened spellbound to my father's rare reminiscences of his RAMC service in Salonika – as remote seeming as the Crimean or Peninsular campaigns. How I have since wished that he had recorded his thoughts and impressions during that campaign. So this is what I have eventually managed to do myself in the 1980s, using my terse diary entries, where still legible, as an *aide memoire*.

The 'long long trail', while fulfilling the notion of war as 'long periods of boredom interrupted by moments of terror' was yet not without rewarding periods of humour and comradeship.

Dummy villa constructed over bunker 0880 Strongpoint

1

On 3 September 1939, when war was declared, I was 25 and engaged to be married. The declaration was no surprise – everyone had come to see it as inevitable. Jean and I were on a cycle tour at the time, starting at Shrewsbury, and we had reached Gloucester when we heard the news of Ribbentrop's Nazi-Soviet pact; then, a little further on the tour, came the news of the attack on Poland.

We had been staying in Youth Hostels and were in the one at Burton Bradstock in Dorset when, unceremoniously, we were asked to leave as the place was being taken over by the Army. In retrospect, we need not have dashed home by train, leaving the cycles to follow; we could have stayed where we were, for this was to prove our last holiday for a long time. But it seemed essential to get back home where my father, a General Practitioner in Formby, Lancashire, was alone in the large house. The rest of the family (my mother, aunt and brothers) were on holiday in Anglesey.

Once home, we spent the time listening to wireless bulletins and organising blackouts for our many large windows; and as it grew dark we turned on all the lights, intending to test the result. Then came yet another news bulletin and we rushed to hear it – forgetting the growing darkness and the curtains, many not yet drawn. A loud banging on the front door broke into the news, and an excited Air Raid Warden announced that the place resembled a lighthouse.

The main excitement in those early days of the war was news of a single German plane over the Firth of Forth. Otherwise nothing happened and it seemed difficult to believe that an epic war had begun. We all started digging in the large garden with vegetable crops in mind, making a midden as compost containers were called in Formby, and we picked and stored all the apples and pears more assiduously than in other years. In fact, there was not much that the ordinary individual could do in the next few months to further the war effort, and once the Germans had overrun Poland very little 'war' seemed to be going on anywhere.

Jean returned to London and after an interval I followed. Later she got a job teaching art in Exeter and I joined the ARP organisation in Chelsea. I was an ambulance driver, mostly on night standby at various stations in Chelsea, but there were no air raids at this time. The pay, however, solved an urgent problem, as there was no other work to be had.

The hiatus between normal peacetime life and real war service – the phoney war period – seemed long and boring. It was clear that I would soon be in one of the services, but the absorption rate was limited by lack of almost everything. It would probably be possible to get into the Infantry as a volunteer Tommy, but nothing more ambitious. My brother, John, had just returned from Palestine where he had been in the police, and he had already joined the Royal Marines in the ranks. I had trained in the Officers Training Corps at school, and having attended camps and passed the proficiency test of Certificate A, I understood that I could get a commission in the Army. But this did not work with the Royal Marines, who I approached at their Whitehall Headquarters.

I cannot remember how I spent off-duty time, but one day I wandered back to the Royal College of Art in Queen's Gate, which I had left in 1936. There I met one of the tutors, Barry Hart, who asked me if I would like to join the Army as a camouflage officer. He had been asked by the War Office to find suitable candidates. This, indeed, seemed a very odd way to enlist a Royal Engineer, for that was the branch of the Army under which the camouflage specialists were to serve, but it was a lucky chance for me that I decided to call at the RCA that day. I was duly interviewed at the War Office, was informed that I would be granted the King's Commission in the Royal Engineers, and was instructed to buy my uniform and hold myself in readiness for posting to the British Expeditionary Force in France.

With my enlistment problem solved and overseas service imminent, I telephoned Jean in Exeter and proposed that we get married as soon as she could get to London. She came, and on 10 February 1940, we shopped for a wedding ring in the King's Road and were married at the Roman Catholic Church in the Fulham Road. My diary records, rather briefly and unromantically:

'Wedding lunch at La Speranza. Jean and I walk in Putney Vale and Richmond Park. Tea Richmond. To Regent Palace Hotel. Rest and bath. To Casino. Show and dance.'

My brother David timed the wedding ceremony on his new stop watch. It was very short. Jean had cyclamen for her bouquet; I was not yet in uniform. Our wedding day was probably typical of so many of the wartime marriages which preceded overseas service.

The few days of our honeymoon are linked in my memory with bewildering communications from the War Office. One was a telegram asking me to resign my Royal Engineers commission as

Wedding photo, outside 'La Speranza' Knightsbridge 10 February 1940

there had been a slip-up; the other was an order to report to the RE
Depot at Chatham in Kent. Here was a dilemma, but on the advice
of my legally-trained brother Michael (aware, no doubt, of the
hazards of once resigning a commission) I telephoned the War
Office and asked which instructions to follow. To my relief I was
told to report to Chatham.

Jean returned to Exeter and I spent the time before reporting to
the RE Depot (on Leap Year Day, 29 February 1940) in trying to
acquire my service dress uniform, Sam Brown belt, cap, etc. I also
had to buy a suitcase – an odd need with which to go to war. I
remember my brother John helping me to get a fake pigskin one
from a lost property office near Victoria.

Reporting at Brompton Barracks, Chatham, was quite an
experience. It was an old and dignified place reeking with

tradition, and the Officers' Mess displayed a wealth of trophies and memorabilia of such eminent sappers as General Gordon of Khartoum.

Newcomers from civil life were treated rather contemptuously by some of the regulars – the Adjutant, in particular, who told me not to wear my great coat like a maternity jacket. The complex webbing equipment was drawn from the Quartermaster and had to be assembled correctly. This caused much puzzlement to other civilians but I was lucky to have become familiar with it at school, also the problem of pipe claying it and polishing the metal.

Some drilling went on, but no sensible co-ordinated training in the use of weapons. I was issued with the standard Army revolver and a few rounds of ammunition, but never had a chance to fire it. A Sapper Officer's outfit included riding breeches in cavalry twill and a very smart navy blue forage cap with the Engineer badge, the bomb embroidered in metal thread. I became very fond of this cap.

In some essentials we were however instructed. For instance, to know the difference between the RE bomb and the RA bomb, the sapper version having two tongues of flame on top of the main bunch. Both badges carried the same motto – *Ubique* (You be Quick). To wear the wrong badge was considered a cardinal sin in either corps and I am sure it still is. The penalty for being spotted with the wrong badge was to stand a round of drinks in the Mess. I liked the notion of a forage cap, presumably a cap to forage in, whatever that may involve; it has a Napoleonic era ring to it.

On 5 March 1940, I spent my embarkation leave in Exeter, where Jean was living with her mother and teaching art at the High School. On the first day we took a picnic lunch to Telegraph Hill and Obelisk Hill, and my diary records, 'Lots of blue birds in ploughed fields. To Dawlish. Bus back in dark.' And another outing on the following day, 'To Exmouth. Walk along shore, promenade and cliffs.' I remember red earth cliffs and a deserted out-of-season forlorn atmosphere.

After returning to the RE Depot at Chatham I spent another fortnight waiting for embarkation orders. During this time I attended a lecture on rifle parts, firing positions and fixing bayonets. I had done all this basic and more advanced training over and over again in the OTC at school, and it would have been better I felt, to have learned something more lethal – grenade throwing or the firing of automatic weapons such as the Bren gun.

At last I received my posting orders – to report to No 693 Artisan Works Company RE 'somewhere in France'. I embarked at Southampton, crossed to Le Havre, and was directed by the troop movement people to somewhere in the Gort Line, up near the Belgian frontier. This proved to be an error and I travelled back to my correct destination on a train packed with locals. It stopped frequently at small stations, and the platforms were full of people eager to board the crowded train, from which no one seemed to be getting off.

As we drew to a halt in one crowded station I noticed a solitary figure in British Army uniform, and after the train was again on its way this British Officer appeared in the corridor, peering into the compartment where I was sitting. When he caught sight of me he forced his way through the sliding door, jammed as it was with standing passengers, and exclaimed in a relieved voice, 'Ah! I was beginning to think there was nobody on the train!'

I duly reported to the 693 Company, RE, which was virtually a conversion of a civil firm into a military unit, stationed on an airfield outside Amiens. The Commanding Officer, a Major, had been the peacetime boss, the Adjutant and Company Officers had been junior administrative staff, the Warrant Officers, NCOs, had been foremen, etc, and the Sappers were supplied from tradesmen and Irish labourers. Not having been trained in such construction work I was rather useless, and made to feel so. However I made up for this by being the only French speaking soldier around, and I was made responsible for the frequent and necessary contact with local farms and such who hired us certain equipment. In this way I met the locals and explored the area. I went to Amiens several times and was able to see the cathedral at leisure. As an artist I was picked on pretty constantly by the CO.

'You're an artist aren't you? OK you can decorate the Mess for our party', and so on. I was also told to buy some reproductions for the Mess – something sentimental or perhaps a bit risqué was indicated. At a shop in Amiens I asked for 'Quelque peintures pour la messe' and was offered a selection of religious pictures, having got the gender of 'messe' wrong. When I finally explained what I wanted, the shop assistant was highly amused.

The party was memorable to me for some typical banter from the CO and an order to do caricatures of all the guests. I was probably tight by then and they turned out rather well or I at least thought they did. One of the guests was a French Officer with a good singing voice who gave a fine rendering of *Ma Normandie*, which has endeared it to me ever since.

This period of my war came to an end in mid-April when I received orders to report to Capt Clark, RE, in a hut near the dock at Port 255 (Calais). He was the Railway Transport Officer and was, I believe, a resident in Calais between the wars, having married a French woman. He was not very welcoming and put me in a small hut on the open ground between the docks and the old town buildings. I was later given an office in one of these, an empty house with an army telephone connecting me to the Chief Engineer's office in Arras, from whom I was to take orders. My job was still connected with the Air Component organisation (as the work on Amiens airfield with 693 had been), and now I was responsible for the onward transport of all equipment sent from England for this airfield programme. The destinations were quite widespread and were known by code names of which I had the key.

The peacetime train ferry vessels were used to transport these varied cargoes, some ready-loaded on rolling stock, some on vehicles, others crated. The details of the cargo were notified by signal just before arrival and I had to obtain destinations from CE Air Component by field telephone. Not being familiar with many of the Sapper activities it was difficult to decipher the often garbled items of equipment on the teleprinter; but I had to read them out intelligibly to the Officer at Arras and note the destination code he gave me – all this over a very crackly telephone line.

The British Officer in charge of the Port arrangements was not Capt Clark (who only concerned himself with movement of personnel) but a very fiery Brigadier of the Royal Marines. I think he was probably appointed to this position because he was over-age. He was well decorated with medals and mustard keen, so the whole operation of docking, passing through the connecting lock into the terminal basin and unloading had to be at the double. This operation was obviously the high point of his service and into it he poured all his vigour and efficiency. Unfortunately the cargoes often arrived in an erratic order so that quick unloading of wagons and transport proved difficult. The loads became the business of the French railways once they landed, and I can still hear the sound of the strange horns they blew as a signal to engine drivers.

For the first two days of my arrival in Calais I stayed in the Excelsior, a very typical French hotel in the old town – in what I believe was regarded as the main street leading across the canal which isolated the old town from the modern area. Later I was billeted with a French family in the new town.

As the train ferry became more and more irregular due to mining of the Channel by the Germans there was plenty of spare time, and I tried to do some sketching, starting with a watercolour of an interesting bright red lightship, which was in a dock for repairs. As I worked I became aware of a knot of people regarding me from a distance. An artist becomes accustomed to being watched and molested while at work in the open, but then some gendarmes arrived and I realised that this was something different. I was surrounded and ordered to follow them to the RTO office. There was much alarm at this stage of the war about Fifth Column activities, but luckily Capt Clark was on duty and cleared me.

That incident cut out my only activity for killing time. Instead I wandered all round the port area, the Old Town and the newer parts, and this reconnaissance was to prove useful later.

I remember a rather disoriented 'Stinker Murdoch' (Richard Murdoch of Radio's *Much Binding in the Marsh*) spending a day or two in Calais on his way to an ENSA programme for the BEF. There was very little British Army involvement with Calais – nearly all troop movements seemed to go to other ports. Indeed the only British troops about were a group of Censorship Officers with whom I used to eat in various cheap cafés and restaurants. I visited some of the railheads on the coded list and had to keep good personal relationships with the Commanding Officers of Sapper companies working in the area.

Among the more mystifying items on the Calais cargo lists were RB-14s and RB-20s, and no one could tell me what to expect. When they arrived they proved to be Ruston Bucyrus excavators, with jibs of various lengths – 14 or 20 feet. For the prompt off-loading of these I had to borrow a driver from an excavating company RE along the coast, but after one or two false alarms when the train ferry had been cancelled, the overworked Sapper companies were unwilling to loan drivers. It became more and more nerve-racking and hard to avoid the wrath of the Brigadier for a hitch in off-loading, so I decided to learn the job myself.

These RBs and their ungainly jibs could cause much damage in the French villages and small towns en route to destinations, for as they turned corners they were liable to swing into the old, narrowly spaced, corner buildings – not to mention the havoc caused among overhead cables and wires.

On 26 April my diary signalled another change in my war career – an interview with Col Beddington, then in charge of the camouflage activities in the BEF. He was friendly and encouraging, with a twinkle in his eye and an urbane manner. I was told that I would shortly be posted back to England to attend a camouflage course and cheered by the prospect of returning to England soon and working in a more rewarding activity, I awaited the move at Port 255. Meanwhile I continued dealing with an irregular and ever-lessening number of train ferries from Harwich.

It is strange to reflect how normal and calm and confident were all these plans in the lull before the German assault on Holland and Belgium, did we but know it, only 12 days away.

News of the blitzkrieg came in radio news bulletins on 12 May, and the writing was clearly on the wall. But still there was general disbelief that a total disaster was imminent. Surely a counter-attack must come – the French, if not the British forces, were huge and thought to be well armed. But day by day the threat got clearer. To us in Calais it seemed a very personal threat.

On 20 May bombers attacked Calais. A flurry of Military Police on motorcycles swept into the town and the place was suddenly full of British troops of all ranks. I had moved back to the Excelsior as the alarm had more or less emptied Calais of civilians, and I volunteered to vacate my room for Gen Ironside – only to be told curtly that the hotel had already been taken over. Shortly after this the Excelsior received a direct hit from a bomb.

I settled into the cellar of a corner house at Rue des Quatre Coins, which was occupied by the Censorship Officers. I left my kit there, and when I came back later they had departed, taking it all with them. The cellar was now occupied by a motley collection of troops cut off from their units.

Earlier, during the bombing, a French Officer had been caught in the open area along the docks and the bomb had spattered him neatly against the wall of a hangar. It was the first corpse I had seen and perhaps the strangest throughout the entire war, because he was not so much a corpse as a splash, but still just human. He had a full ceremonial funeral nevertheless, a real French ceremony with a band, plumed black-draped horses and everything.

The next day, as there was now no more dock work to do (ferries having ceased) I begged a lift to Boulogne on an RAMC convoy, hoping to catch up with the Censorship Officers who were said to have moved there, taking my kit with them – my 'pig-skin' suitcase containing all my treasures, including 21st birthday presents and some paintings. We had to evacuate the civil hospital at Abbeville and the journey was slow due to vast hordes of French and Belgian refugees pouring westwards – pedestrians and families in heavily mattress-covered cars and farm carts. The general French exodus started at about this time, whereas the flight of refugees from Belgium and Holland had started earlier.

How great a change from the earlier complacency during the gathering storm! When I first saw the Dutch troops I thought they were German prisoners due to their grey uniforms and the shape of their steel helmets. A mere day or two before I had gone to the part of Calais where the main east-west road passed through, to watch troop convoys going east, including some significantly out-dated items such as a carrier pigeon unit – a rather pretty cavalcade which was warmly applauded by the excited onlookers. I had a strong feeling of embarrassment when refugees from Belgium, seeing my British uniform, started clapping and singing *Tipperary*.

Boulogne was in a ferment – full of British Army evacuating. I parted from the ambulance convoy after arranging to meet them by the dock in the evening for the return to Calais. I actually managed to trace the flight of the Censorship Officers and discovered they had vacated a building now occupied by a medical unit – but my suitcase was there. Finding was one thing, removing it was another, and I was hauled before a very wild looking RAMC Colonel who informed me that he had just had a Fifth Columnist shot. He ordered me to prove myself. I could only show my identity card but could produce no one to vouch for me and I suddenly felt very vulnerable – not from the approaching Germans but from the panic on my own side.

Eventually I was allowed to go, hugging my suitcase from which the strap had broken, and somehow I spent the day in Boulogne awaiting the return of the ambulance convoy. In the existing atmosphere of unreality and panic, with rumours that the Germans had reached the coast and were just outside Boulogne itself, the restaurants were, surprisingly, still open. A large flight of fighters went over, and for a moment they were assumed to be Spitfires, but their identity was soon declared when they bombed the dock area.

No RAMC convoy appeared, although I waited hopefully long past the agreed time. All around me, as I waited, were untidily parked British Army vehicles, and it dawned on me that they were abandoned – that I had better take one and get back to Calais where I was at least known to a handful of my own side. Rather shamefacedly I tried to start one vehicle after another, realising to my dismay that they had been immobilised, probably as a futile gesture by their fleeing owners. Eventually I got a saloon car to start up with a heartening but unnaturally loud roar. There seemed to be no way of controlling the speed of the engine, but at least it went.

I had spoken to a Lieutenant in charge of a small group of still-manned Signal Corps vehicles, and he had said that later on he was going to Calais. I asked if I could travel with him but he seemed doubtful, and once more I had the uneasy feeling that I was under suspicion. Enemy aircraft were again over Boulogne, and as I watched the Signal Corps pull out I decided to get going on my own. My car bolted through the medieval gate and soon I was outside the town on the straight tree-lined road leading to Calais.

The only way to slow the speed of the car was to depress the clutch and let the engine roar. Otherwise it was a case of full out or switch off and stop. I was too occupied with controlling the vehicle to take much stock of outside events, but suddenly I saw as in a film or a dream, a series of explosions outlining the road ahead, and then a low flying plane roared over. I saw a stationary convoy of Signals vehicles pulled over on to the verge and glimpsed British troops peering out from the shallow ditch alongside, so I switched off and pulled up beyond them, then doubled back to ask if I could join the convoy. It was clearly not healthy to be alone, for the oncoming refugees were showing increasing signs of wanting to stop me and take over the vehicle.

The soldiers I spoke to referred me to the officer further down the ditch, and he turned out to be the Lieutenant I had spoken to in Boulogne. He demanded to see my identity card (which I had produced several times earlier) but I could not find it. As I groped through all the buttoned pockets of my uniform a whistle sounded and they all ran out to their vehicles and started up.

I waited a while, relieved that my lack of an identity card had not been more fully questioned, and started up my car with another roar. In no time I was overtaking the Signal Corps convoy due to my 'all out' speed, and the Lieutenant once more regarded me with a puzzled expression. There were no more aircraft scares but getting through the throng of refugees and cars, carts and people became almost impossible, particularly with no means of driving slowly.

As I approached Calais and saw huge columns of black smoke I wondered if it was such a good idea to be returning, and it was with relief that I switched off outside the Rue des Quatre Coins house. The door was locked and when I banged on it a voice from inside asked me to identify myself. Here we go again, I thought, but after mentioning the names of some of the other inmates and units, I was eventually admitted. Everything had changed, the place was full of strange faces, but there were at least one or two who knew me.

By the next day food problems were arising, for there had never been any British Army messes in Calais and we had come to depend on eating in French restaurants; but now the civilian population had shut houses and businesses and faded away to the south-west. The one exception was a small Salvation Army hut run by a Captain and a lady helper. I had been there for odd snacks and had got to know and like them, for the atmosphere was very easy with no aura of doing good. Now they too were withdrawing, leaving their provisions behind, and I felt justified in removing some of these for survival until I myself received orders to leave Calais. I remember that the main part of my haul consisted of chocolate peppermint bars – very welcome at Quatre Coins, but one soon craved a less exotic diet.

My diary for 23 May reads, 'Guide Officers to places in Calais'. This actually involved conducting a Naval demolition party to some key installations on the outskirts of Calais. Since no one knew how near the Germans were and the area seemed deserted it was rather scary, particularly as the only offensive weapon I had was still my pistol issued at Chatham and about a dozen rounds of ammunition. One lorry load of yelling French soldiers and civilians passed us, heading for Calais Centre.

We now embarked on the demolitions – with total lack of success for it turned out that the detonators were the wrong type, so we returned to the quayside. Here a naval yacht – in fact only a motor-powered yacht with a Commander RN and a small crew – was moored alongside the Gare Maritime, and although small and the Naval touch minimal (the dress of the crew struck a rather piratical note) it was a considerable comfort to know it was there; at least they would acknowledge me. I was offered a meal on board which I very gratefully accepted.

My next job was driving the remaining RBs into the dock, obviously an ineffective gesture which would only delay their use by the Germans -- and nerve racking because my driving knowledge resulted in a trial and error use of the many controls which could have sent me into the dock myself. Towards dusk a long hospital train pulled into one of the marshalling areas situated near the Gare Maritime, and when shelling started we wondered how they would fare. Two cargo ships had also arrived in Calais, and these had discharged troops and Bren carriers which moved off to the Calais perimeter.

I made myself useful in various rather meaningless ways and eventually went down to the cellars under the Gare Maritime for the night where holiday posters still covered the station buildings. During the night I witnessed a remarkable little conference in the cellar. An exhausted soldier of the East Yorks Regiment was stretched on a large table, dead to the world – probably one of many who had made their long and solitary retreat into Calais from some disastrous delaying action. At the end of the table sat a Canadian General, other Canadian Officers and the Naval Commander from the yacht. In a strangely matter of fact way the

General was attempting to assess the military situation from scraps of fact and opinion which the others were scarcely able to supply. I got the impression that he was hoping there would be a case for bringing his Canadian Division over to counter-attack.

Fortunately decisions were taken on sounder intelligence elsewhere, and the Canadians were not committed to what would surely have been an even worse disaster. The British force which had landed and was at this time engaged on the permimeter was later a total loss. They had no chance. I had earlier met a school friend, Simon Molloy, and officer in the Queen Victoria Rifles, and had a few words with him before he moved off to the perimeter – and a Prisoner of War camp for the rest of the war.

During that night and at first light the shelling intensified and proved uncannily accurate, putting some of the dockside cranes out of action. These had been operated by French civilians who had largely disappeared. It was said afterwards that the German artillery had been in telephonic communication with Fifth Column observers in the town, who reported the accuracy of the shelling over the civilian telephone service.

I was woken abruptly at 4.30 am and summoned to help transfer wounded to the *Ben Lawers* from the hospital train which had moved alongside the quay from the marshalling yard. The men had been wounded in Belgium and had been in the train some days, being shunted this way and that to avoid the German advance. The *Ben Lawers* was a medium-sized cargo ship which, with the *Kohistan*, had brought in the Queen Victoria Rifles and their vehicles and ammunition, as yet only half off-loaded.

When I first emerged from the stuffy cellar and instinctively sniffed the fresh salt air I was met with, for me, a new and very unpleasant smell. It was the smell of scorched flesh, coming from the corpses of men who had received direct hits on the quayside. For the unloading of the hospital train it was a question of pairing off with someone, going into the train (which also stenched heavily) and carrying to the ship a wounded man on his stretcher. Very soon all the available space below decks was full, and stretchers had to be arranged on the open decks. Shelling had become, for some reason, less heavy, and I can remember standing by the rail of the *Ben Lawers*, looking down on the quay at the heaps of covered corpses and a mass of kit and equipment abandoned by troops who had left previously.

I had at last improved my personal armament by picking up an abandoned rifle with which I was comfortably familiar, and my main concern now was to be aboard the ship and not on the quay when the moment came to pull out. This happened at 6.30 am, which was the latest the ship could make it out of the harbour on the falling tide. My relief when I felt the gentle slow movement of the ship from the quay was overwhelming – but clouded by a sense of the great disaster in which I had been involved.

Directly the ship cleared the harbour it came under shell fire from the French coastal battery at Sangatte (about 8,000 yards along the coast to the west) which the Germans had taken over. One shell ricochetted off the sea and bounced into an open Bren carrier – but failed to explode. We passed British destroyers heading for Calais and were soon out of range of France. On this beautiful May morning the English coast was clearly visible, as it had been for most of the last few days, tantalisingly close and inviting. At last we were on our way and leaving behind the mad chaos that had overtaken us in France.

Very soon we were lying off Dover, the town stretched out peacefully under a bright sun but with a very full harbour. Pilot boats sailed to and fro and we expected every minute to put in and start unloading the casualties who were clearly in a bad way, the RAMC being completely exhausted and supplies of drugs running out. However, after an anxious four hour wait, and shouted converstations from the Captain to the pilot boat, it was obvious that we would not be allowed to put into an already overcrowded Dover. So we put to sea again.

There were no adequate rations on board and the problem of food returned. The Captain and ship's Officers were British and the rest of the crew Lascar seamen. It was intensely cold on deck and the main holds foul with the stench of the wounded. There was one small room, part of the ship's crew quarters, and here a mixture of fit troops assembled for warmth. The Lascars served some very weak fish soup and, hungry as we were, it tasted good. Sleep was impossible as there was no space to lie down.

A number of French troops were on board, which caused some awkward situations when the disaster was discussed and the performance of the French forces was sourly criticised. I felt that this was possibly well-founded opinion, but to pretend that anything other than the 20-odd miles of Channel had saved the British forces was hypocritical.

We reached Southampton on the morning of 25 May and docked at 4 am. The first to go ashore (carried down a very steep gangplank) were a number of corpses covered with Union Jacks – casualties who had not survived the voyage. Then the Southampton ARP took over the task of carrying down the several hundred wounded. Four hours later the fit me were allowed ashore. We were told that there would be a field cashier available in the dockside shed to provide some ready money and we were not allowed to leave that shed until midday.

I was wearing my service dress uniform, a trench coat and a steel helmet. I still had my pistol, but now had also a Lee Enfield rifle and some bandoliers of .303 ammunition – otherwise nothing. I was dirty and unshaven. The others were all in the same state, and it was obvious that we were an embarrassment to the authorities. The debacle in France was not yet being made public – the 'miracle' of Dunkirk was still in the future. We had to do our best to pass unnoticed and say nothing of our experiences.

The train journey to Aldershot was unforgettable. 'Country looks heavenly' I noted in my diary – beautiful and peaceful after the scenes of recent days. Hawthorn in full bloom was profuse in the hedges and everywhere was the lushest, greenest grass imaginable. There was such normality and peace that the horror of Calais seemed a bad dream.

At Aldershot we went to a tented camp. I was restless to let Jean and my family know that I was back, and I took the line with the RTO that I must report direct back to AG7 at the War Office. This surprisingly worked; I got a travel warrant and took the next train to London, making my way to where Jean was staying in a house near Gloucester Road. She was out – a sad anticlimax – but there was a bunch of Australian girls there who showed great excitement when they discovered who I was.

I went to my brother Michael's flat and, welcomed by his wife Dorothy, had one of the best baths in my life. Then Jean arrived – after being mysteriously dolled up (without being told the reason) by the Australians. We celebrated our reunion with a meal at Nic's in the King's Road, Chelsea, and then went back to Gloucester Road. That night Jean told me I had nightmares and shouted 'Follow me, men'. I rather doubt that I wanted to lead them back into France – and anyway I had no men! We lunched next day at La Speranza, the restaurant where we had our wedding lunch 15 strange weeks earlier.

By the end of May I was posted to Willsworthy, Devon. This was a wonderful release, a tented camp in lovely peaceful country on the edge of Dartmoor. Jean was making the most of this break after all that had happened, and she came down to stay at Lydford, the nearest small Devonshire village. There was very little the troops could do, for everything in the form of equipment was in short supply and units were mixed up and depleted. I was given the job of

14

painting the white bell tents in the camp with cutch, a dark brown stain, plus I did bouts of duty officer.

There was a good deal of freedom. The world was crashing, but it was, as the contemporary song said, 'the first weekend in June'; the weather was beautiful, there were strawberries and cream, and Jean and I were together again.

This period was only clouded by an ever blackening series of news bulletins. The full horror of the time was, however, brought home to us when we were moved out of Willsworthy to make way for the remnants of a Black Watch unit direct from Dunkirk. They simply lay down and slept.

2

On 12 June 1940, I received orders from AG7 at the War Office to join No 2 Camouflage Course at the Royal Artillery Camp (A Mess) at Larkhill on Salisbury Plain. I arrived on 13 June with my few belongings in a brown paper parcel, still not having been issued with new kit. This was, I think, the second camouflage course, chiefly under the control of Maj Buckley, RE, who had a Military Cross from the 1914-18 War and wore a crisp military moustache with neat tufts of hair on his cheeks.

My brief overseas experience served rather to antagonise Maj Buckley, whose First World War service had up till then been regarded as the latest authentic experience. Now he seemed to feel the need to defer to me and ask if, in fact, it was still the same in this war. But I knew nothing about the normality of modern war from the unreal goings on in and around Calais.

Other recently commissioned officers on the course included John Hutton, artist; Peter Proud, film art director; and Bainbridge Copnall, sculptor. After a series of lectures the course moved to London for demonstrations at the Denham film studios covering plaster moulding and other scenic film techniques which it was thought would prove useful in dummy construction – and indeed they did during the scramble programme of pill box construction, concealment and disguise in the anxious months following Dunkirk. A further week at Larkhill brought the course to an end on 29 June.

Jean had followed me to Wiltshire from Devon and had found lodgings in Amesbury, a few miles from the camp; so we both returned to London and on 1 July I went back to Chatham, where postings of the officers from No 2 Camouflage Course were made known. Mine was to HQ 7th Anti-Aircraft Division, Gosforth House, Newcastle. At this low point in the war there were no true active operational areas other than the Western Desert.

The 7th AA Div HQ was located in the parkland of the old Gosforth House, east of the Great North Road as it left Newcastle. Jean and I rented a flat, and her mother came to join us shortly afterwards.

The duties of a camouflage officer with an Ack Ack division were quite taxing and diverse. I had to get to know all the heavy and light gun sites in an area concentrated mainly around Newcastle and along the coast, but also including Northumberland, Durham and Yorkshire. Having visited the gun sites, ammunition dumps and other installations, and done what one could to organise effective camouflage, it was necessary to wangle flights from local RAF stations to check the effect from the air. This was often difficult to achieve as there were no readily available aircraft for the purpose. Untoward incidents happened to me so often that I wondered if any flight would ever be quite normal from take off to landing.

Excerpts from:
7th AA Division Operation Orders   1 August 1940

General Remarks
All bombing attacks must start from a high altitude (7000ft upwards). Even dive bombers must approach and locate target at considerable height and some distance before the actual dive can start. It is therefore patent that concealment from observation at 7000ft will go far to frustrate all types of attack.

Methods to bring about concealment
a   By imitation of non-military objects
b   By imitation of natural vegetation

Colour and tone
Experience proves that at over 5000ft it is tone and not colour which differentiates object . . . further accentuated by the shape of their shadows. At high altitude colour dissolves into more or less light and shade, and surface roughness (texture) causes tone shade variation and obliterates fine lines.

Example At 5000ft a rough green surface can appear darker than a flat smooth black surface.

Reason A rough field of grass does not reflect much light and appears dark because the myriads of blades intermingle their shadows, whereas a patch of trodden black earth reflects, and so appears light.
    Thus concrete surfaces always appear comparatively light even if coloured dark because they are smooth. They must not only be darkened, but also roughened and their margins broken.
    Trees contain so much shadow within their foliage that all woods appear dark or black at 3000ft.
    Tracks spoil (freshly turned earth) and sandbags appear very light and conspicuous. They are smooth and reflect the light.

Situation
It is of vital importance to put into operation a general scheme of

camouflage now . . . it is proposed that the work be undertaken in two stages:–

a   to render all sites as inconspicuous as possible at once, priority, being given to AA sites defending Aerodromes and other VPs.

b   A more individual treatment for the concealment from the air of defensive sites as far as possible.

Siting

Where new sites or resiting are contemplated, Brigade should notify Divisional Camouflage Officer so that he may advise as to the scheme or camouflage before work is started and track worn. A vacated site may be dressed up as a dummy.

Duties of Divisional Camouflage Officer

1 To advise Units on all matters concerning Camouflage.

2 To report to Divisional Headquarters all cases of inadequate camouflage work at sites.

3 To consult with RE authorities responsible for effecting Camouflage schemes.

Signed   S. B. Sykes
2/Lt RE
7th AA Divisional Camouflage Officer

CAMOUFLAGE MATERIALS – general

Paint Provision of materials and arrangements for work by civil contract under CREs will be responsibility of the latter.

Artillery nets and scrim

a   A certain number of Artillery Extension nets 17 × 35 are at present available. Scrim (coloured hessian strips) is also available. Allotment scale of scrim is four rolls per net various colours – dark green and grass green, dark and light brown loam.

b   To conform with present supply units should indent . . . the following scale of allotment:–

Light AA Units	5 nets per gun
Heavy AA Units	5 nets per gun
S/L Units	4 nets per site

General rules and hints

1 Parapets

All parapets constructed by Units themselves should be darkened at once. On flattened sandbags, paint alone will not be effective, and recourse must be had to surface roughening and breaking up of regular shape.

2 Mounding

Mounding of earth from grounding to parapet should be as gradual as possible, and should be very rough as it shows light from the air. Mounding properly done eliminates shadow. This can also be achieved by netting.

3 Floors

Mud carried into gun pits by troops boots will make a black surface light very rapidly. Site Officers should see that reasonable care is taken and mud washed out regularly.

Clinker and ashes dust may cause damage to instruments but chippings and shingle are satisfactory, provided they are continually darkened with paint.

4 Tracks

All photos show clearly that Tracks and Spoil are by far the most serious problems of site concealment.

Treatment of tracks

a   Make use of, or imitate existing non-military tracks. Diagonal tracks in fields are particularly conspicuous, and where unavoidable may be continued beyond the site to a reasonable destination. Site Officers must enforce strict track discipline and detail alternative routes to be used, if possible following hedgerow, roads, etc.

b   Tracks may be camouflaged as a hedge by covering with clinker or other dark material, tar or bitumen. Experience shows that width must be 12ft and edges should be boldly curved and jagged.

5 Roads concrete

The best method of dealing with concrete is to cover with coarse granite or whinstone chips . . . and to spray with colour where necessary.

6 Tentage

All white tentage must be painted dark green at once. It may be applied with brush or sprayed, and the work is better accomplished by the latter method with the tent struck, and the operateor keeping to windward. Tents should be sited irregularly, and full advantage taken of hedgerows, copses and woods.

7 Guns

Guns should be painted with Anti-Gas paint (except for working surfaces which should be oiled).

8 MT or AFVs

All vehicles when parked must be
a   Widely and irregularly dispersed when on open ground.
b   Amply covered with natural foliage whenever possible.
c   Parked so as to profit by all cover of trees and hedges in shadows of buildings.

I remember one flight to reconnoitre some recent camouflage work on heavy gun sites near Newcastle. The plane was a Fairey Battle – very little heard of during the war, and presumably a failure. It was rather a beautiful plane, however, with a very long covered section extending backwards from the pilot to the navigator, known as the greenhouse. I was placed in this centre point, lying face downwards over an open hatch (used to observe and presumably to bomb). We flew at several thousand feet and it was very cold. I began to pick out the various gun sites disappointingly easily – the typical gun site signature of the four emplacements, command post and connecting tracks stood out readily against all the other complex patterns, urban, semi-urban and rural.

Suddenly a warning buzzer sounded and I looked forward to the pilot who was making a thumbs-down sign. I was trying to work out what this signified and what I was supposed to do when the plane went into a vertical dive, not pulling out till near the ground. I held on somehow, mentally and physically, and was still holding on rigidly when we landed and the crew asked me rather dubiously if I was all right. I was far from all right – frozen, feeling sick with panic, but with my pride as a soldier among airmen, I said I was OK. They then explained that a flight of Free Czech Airforce Hurricanes had been on our tail and evidently about to attack. The Fairey Battle, being a relatively rare British plane, was liable to be confused with the enemy Junkers, and the sudden dive was the pilot's answer to the problem.

Camouflage duties nearer home involved disguise for a typical hexagonal concrete pill box sited in the park for the defence of the HQ itself. To make a good job of this could have valuable propaganda results with the HQ staff and the General himself, so I went to work on a summer house disguise – a relatively simple operation but highly praised by the Division Commander.

Meanwhile the pre-planning of the gun sites in a sensible and effective way was not progressing too well. I wondered afterwards how important this really was, or indeed practically possible. The main give-away of a typical layout (ideal for the operation of the guns) was hard to combat. From the air the service tracks stood out like chalked signatures. Equal efforts expended in the construction of dummy or decoy sites would have been more profitable and were used in due course. But this period of my war was to be brought to a sudden end on 28 November 1940, when I received a posting order which read:

Lieut S. B. Sykes RE Staff Lieut (Cam) selected for appointment of Staff Lieut (Cam) HQ Western Desêrt, Middle East. Instruct him to be ready to proceed at short notice. Embarkation orders will be issued by QM 1B.

The bits that struck home were 'Western Desert' and 'at short notice' – exciting to go to this battle front where things were actually happening, and the Italians were proving reasonably satisfactory opposition, but also daunting in its unguessable outcome.

I was granted embarkation leave, and Jean and I cleared up our belongings. We saw Jean's mother off to relations in Somerset, and travelled home to Formby. There we found my brother Michael on leave with his wife Dorothy, and their very young daughter, Ann. He was on leave from Catterick where he was training, quite unsuitably, in the Royal Corps of Signals. And as I was not expecting to be around on 25 December, we had our Christmas dinner on the 12th instead. Then I returned to Newcastle and on by night train to London.

There followed brief and not very profitable visits to the Army Camouflage Training and Development Centre at Farnham Castle, Surrey, and then I went on to Warwickshire to the Civil Defence Camouflage Centre in Leamington. Other camouflage officers from the Larkhill course had also been posted to the Middle East and I met them again on these visits. Everyone seemed to be on the move and the Blitz was on in London. I have a mental picture at this time of long delayed blacked-out trains and stations and endless goings and comings to courses, leaves, postings and partings.

Jean and I managed after all to spend Christmas together in Formby (although I spent all Christmas Day on the train). I bought Jean a suitcase for her birthday on 27 December, and the next few days consisted of a succession of trivial events. They indicate the need to keep doing familiar, normal, unremarkable things up to the last day. One occupation was shopping for a topee (included in my kit list); I searched the whole of Liverpool unsuccessfully for this, only to find my father's uniform *and topee* from the First World War in the dressing-up cupboard at Formby!

In this cupboard there were costumes for gnomes, Mickey Mouse, Red Devil and other childhood favourites, and these I remember being made by a lady who came in to sew when we were very small. We were allowed to choose a costume from Weldon's *Illustrated Catalogue of Patterns*. They always looked much more convincing in the illustrations than the rather thin, limp cotton garments and caps which were made for us. In the cupboard there were also odds and ends from various sources – furs, capes and obsolete articles of fashion, but also some bits of my father's uniform from the First World War – and there, sure enough, was his Salonika campaign topee. The diary records, 'It will do – also khaki shorts.'

My departure day was cold and frosty. Packing was completed, and goodbyes were said to all. Then Jean and I departed for Gladstone Dock and, for me, *RMS Samaria*. Jean could not come beyond the Dock gate – and there we parted. I found my cabin and two of my cabin mates, both camouflage officers, Fielding and Wilton (the latter ex regular Infantry); the third, who I met later, was Alexander, 16/5 Lancers. Other camouflage officers on board included Peter Proud, Robert Medley, John Codner and Jasper Maskelene, the internationally renowned stage magician.

The ship was very hot and stuffy but intensely cold on deck, from which there were drab views of the dock and greasy water. I had tea and dinner, read *The Seven Pillars of Wisdom*, and then looked at the Plough at 10 o'clock. I had a pact with Jean for both of us to look at the stars of the Plough every night at 10 pm. Obviously some difficulties were going to develop over this – the change in time, for one, but it was a comfort in its way.

The next morning we were still alongside Gladstone Dock and still overlooking the same drab sheds, cranes and foul water. It was misty and cold, with icicles. I wrote to Jean and caught the 2 pm post; then at 3 o'clock, at last, we moved away from the dock. It was a very unromantic departure with only disinterested dock hands as witnesses, though one of them, standing alone, looked more concerned than the rest and gave us the thumbs up. We halted opposite the larger *Empress of Australia* – full of the Royal Air Force – and for a while the two huge bulks faced each other with thousands of faces staring across and shouting cracks at each other like football supporters. Then we wheeled round and saw much more colour and interest – about a dozen destroyers and sloops becomingly camouflaged in shades of grey, blue and pink. Adjacent docks had been badly blitzed, drooping cranes giving them a melted look. We anchored in mid Mersey, but the light was failing and no familiar Liverpool landmarks were visible.

On 7 January, the third day of the voyage, the *Samaria* finally moved out of the Mersey. It was strange to be leaving from Liverpool of all ports, for it meant passing within sight of the shore at Formby. I could pick out the Hall Road sea front and the Altcar

Rifle Range flag, but it was dusk and very dim. There was a lifetime of memories evoked by that strange flat coastline where the tide comes and goes nearly a mile and the pale marram-covered sandhills are backed by black pine woods. The only buildings were one or two isolated Victorian houses half buried in the sand, the drifting sand defying the schemes of developers – much to the benefit of Formby dwellers.

It would have been a remarkable and neat departure if that hazy glimpse of my own local shore had also indeed been my 'last of old England'. But we were not on our way, far from it, and we anchored again in the light of a half moon.

By the next day we were lying off what I took to be Wales – Puffin Island, the Great Orme and the snow-covered slopes of the Snowdon range. Notable ships in the convoy besides the *Empress of Australia*, were *Munster*, *Brittanic*, *Windsor Castle*, and also a zebra striped destroyer, three Hurricanes and a flying boat. Later, with the help of a map, I was able to recognise Red Wharf Bay, Cemaes Bay, and the top of Holyhead Mountain, white cottages and houses, and the beloved little fields of Anglesey. The memories packed into the Formby and Freshfield shores, and Anglesey summer holidays, were endless.

The Camouflage Pool (unattached officers) were appointed to units – mine being A Section 1003 Docks Group Company RE, and our time was occupied with talks to troops on such subjects as water supply difficulty, how going short would make us 'pukka men by the time we get to the east'. More ships joined the convoy at Belfast Lough, and we had a concert in the Warrant Officers' Mess. I was starting a cold and beginning to feel ill.

By the end of the first week the convoy had doubled in size and we were really starting to move. Twenty large liners and seven or eight escorts – impressive, but what a target! We speeded up and left Mull of Kintyre to the right, Ratlin Island to the left, and through field glasses I watched a very lovely moon rise, its crusted surface remarkably clear.

I was appointed ship's Orderly Officer, with all the inspections and supervisions that post involves – inspect and post guard, make round of men's Mess rooms, visit sentries, turn out guard and inspect prisoners (six). I did a round with ship's officers of the watch. The mens' quarters were one solid mass of hammocks, some men sleeping on the floor and on tables. There was very little air, lots of dirt and untidy mess to be seen to. They were all eating, living and sleeping in the same cramped quarters. I visited the bakery and galleys, and then had a very bad night in the orderly room sleeping on a stretcher. My cold was getting worse, finally settling into an inflamed antrum.

Our OC gave us more talks. His style was to brush lightly from one well tried sentiment to another, with much emphasis on 'the big family', 'my boys', what Hitler and Mussolini won't understand, and still how the water shortage would make us 'pukka men'. I felt very ill by now, with an infected sinus and nothing to be done other than swallow aspirins and inhale. The doctor was an ENT (ear, nose and throat) man but had no equipment to operate. The pain came in a 24 hour cycle and I stayed in the sweaty cabin for some days. My camouflage friends, Robert Medley and Peter Proud, lent me books and a portable gramophone, and I played *L'ombre s'enfuit*, sung by Tino Rossi, endlessly. Tropical kit was adopted on 20 January, 16 days from freezing Liverpool.

On day 19 of the voyage my father's honoured Salonika topee sadly came to an unworthy end. It was of a different pattern to the current official issue and looked more appropriate for a missionary than a soldier. I came in for some good natured but rough ragging about it, and the 'pugree' began to unwind as it was tossed about. Eventually it went over the stern of the ship and became a target for gunnery practice. Inwardly I mourned its inglorious end. I was issued with a more modern but less nostalgic version.

Two days later the convoy went into single file and the mountains of Sierra Leone became visible. We docked at Freetown at 8 am but failed to get ashore. I had my first Arabic lesson at this time from Freddie Beeston, and progress was rather cheering, the utter impossibility of the thing not seeming so great as I had anticipated. Beeston was a very likeable Intelligence Corps Officer, bespectacled and owl-like, who knew classical Arabic from university days, but he had never been to an Arabic speaking country. He took great pains with us. The *Seven Pillars of Wisdom* had inspired me to emulate Lawrence, and to speak Arabic seemed an essential step.

On 29 January we left Freetown, and once at sea again boat drill, Arabic and PT became the order of the day. February marked the end of our first month aboard; one man died of sunstroke. Then, on 11 February, the convoy moved single file into Durban, and the rumour of shore leave proved correct. I changed notes for silver which was legal tender, and with Medley wandered along the esplanade as it became dark and the lights came on – a moment of magic after the blackouts at home and on the ship. We looked for a small restaurant, which we couldn't find, for all eating seemed to be done in the grill rooms of large hotels. Then we met a Sergeant of the South African Army who took us to the Yacht Club for drinks.

The South Africans were very kind and hospitable, and the next day Robert Medley and I were invited by a Mr Cairns to dinner at his home in Malvern (10 miles out). In the meantime we had coffee and a bathe – lovely bands of colour in the sea, with pink near the shore, gay sunshades, and the sand so scorching that you had to hop from foot to foot. The next day Wilton hired a car and we drove out to the Blue Lagoon, where we had tea in the open on a lawn by the shore. There were bright flowers, cream and scones and jam and music. We drove on over Umgene and finally, by devious routes, reached the Umslunga Rocks Hotel.

Wilton astonished me with his accurate deja vu guesses as to the character of the country in every detail – uncanny, I thought, until he later revealed that he had taken the same route on the previous day! Above all I remember the delight of being in a car – not a troopship. I was grateful to Carl Wilton for letting me join him while he careered around in his hired car, but the restrictions of the route left me with an impatient longing to see more of the vast country that lay to the north, all the way to Cairo.

That evening some of the restaurants were closed owing to Australian rioting. Sad to relate, the Australians from the convoy had rioted and killed and been killed in the nether regions of Durban. They had done something very tough here in the 1914-18 War and had, it seems, a tradition to uphold.

By the time we left Durban we were sad to go. We had been entertained by South Africans, had shopped, bathed and visited the Snake Park – and generally we had begun to relate to the place in many ways. The Snake Park left a vivid memory, horrifying yet irresistible. I have a personal snake phobia, and the pits of varied deadly snakes were not, it seemed to me, very well caged.

Our ship was the last to sail and it was tantalising to see the rest of the convoy go out, giving their three hoots and being sent off by enthusiastic crowds. But we sailed at last, with a stirring farewell from all the kind people gathered to see us off; and how lovely and desirable the place and our new acquaintances seemed as they grew rapidly more distant. Then everything was back to normal, leaving us rather unsettled. Having tasted avocado pears for the first time in Durban, I was delighted to find that a supply had been taken on board and was on the ship's menu.

We were now back to normal trooping routine, working on Arabic and sleeping on deck; but at last I was feeling fit again, with no more sinus trouble. We had a Lewis gun course, shooting at boxes slotted off the stern of the ship. I had trained with Lewis guns at school and had regarded them as a remnant of the First World War which would have given way to Brens, Stens, etc. However, they seemed pretty effective. Time was advanced again one hour, playing hell with the 10 pm look for the Plough. Wilton and I had agreed to do the scenery for the ship's pantomime, and now I got roped in for the job of wardrobe master. I painted a paper wig for the princess and helped Medley with a turban.

Day 52 of the voyage was Beeston's birthday and I had dinner and wine at his table, with chess afterwards. A few days later we were off Kamaran Island – very sheer and bleak. Lectures on Vickers MG were followed by officers' night at the pantomime. Very hot and a bit wearisome, though there were some bright spots and one catchy song, an alternative *White Cliffs of Dover* composed on board.

On 3 March we woke to a rather grand view of precipitous hills to port, pale and very bare, then a dull low coastline with some much higher and more exciting peaks rising behind, almost lost and very atmospheric in the haze. Finally, at about 5 o'clock we arrived at the head of the Gulf, amidst a mass of shipping. It was a lovely evening with the hills a tawny colour and very bare. There was not much town visible – a few square blocks of houses and oil tanks at a distance. A feeling of excitement at having arrived spread through the ship and general festivities developed – including football in the lounge!

Anticlimax followed and was rather shattering – apparently the result of the Commander of the Shock (landing) ship convoy having blown up at the sight of such a close concentration of ships. We were just within reach of long range Axis aircraft from across the Mediterranean. We continued to lie, for several days, dispersed offshore some miles back down the Gulf.

Arabic lessons continued, and here I must say a few words about our Arabic tutor, Freddie Beeston – who for some reason got the nickname Huku (derived from the Arabic word for government, hukumatu, if I remember rightly). When, on 9 March at Port Tewfik, we first came face to face with live Arabs over the side of the *Samaria*, we all waited with bated breath for Huku to converse with them. He was a bit shy with such an audience, but spoke out bravely. The fellaheen were halted in their tracks. We all thought his words were proving incomprehensible – but not a bit of it. They were astonished into silence by the pure classic style of speech coming from this rotund Englishman. It was, I suppose, as if the

26

stevedores of a British port were addressed by a foreigner in pure Chaucerian, or perhaps Shakespearean, English.

1003 Company went ashore at Port Tewfik and I got leave to follow them principally as they had taken my kit with them. Why my kit was always the one to be picked up by mistake was a mystery, but I got it back and had drinks in an Officers' Club overlooking the sea at the entrance to the canal.

Day 65 was the last on the *Samaria* and at 3.45 pm we boarded the train to Cairo, where Beeston, Neville, Wilton and I booked in at the National Hotel, Beeston and I sharing a room. We went out to see the city, and called at the Continental where Proud and the others were staying.

This account seems very dry when I think of the terrific impact Cairo made after a 65 days' voyage. It seemed the true East, with its sounds, scents and scenes, with new tastes like halva, which I had bought on the journey, and the Arabic food. Cairo had a heady sophisticated side and a colourful squalor, all intermingled.

3

Immediately on arrival in Cairo we – all the new draft officers – met our Middle East boss, Col G. de G. Barkas, MC (First War), and the next day he took us to the camouflage training ground. Barkas had already been in Cairo for some time and had comprehensive and clear ideas about how he was to use us all in the various commands and zones of operation. During the 65 days of our voyage from Liverpool, Western Desert Force had gone from strength to strength in its campaign against the Italians and had now reached Benghazi. The Germans, on the other hand, were about to launch an attack on Greece, Mussolini's effort against the Greeks, from Albania, having bogged down.

I hoped to be selected to join the Force being put together for Greece and was disappointed to be posted to Palestine. My disappointment proved misplaced, for our expeditionary force, including Clough, Blair Hughes Stanton and the other Camouflage Officers who went to Greece, were all captured.

One of our tasks in the Cairo area was to instruct local contractors in making camouflage nets. Our Arabic learned from the classical Beeston was not much help, but I found the Egyptian workmen had a good sense of humour and we got things moving well.

Col Barkas was meanwhile compiling a very overdue Army manual on *Concealment in the Field*. The average soldier had quite misguided ideas on camouflage and little comprehension of its real possibilities and limitations. For instance, units arrived with camouflage nets garnished in greens and browns suited to European landscapes and, as good disciplinarians, they had pegged them out stiffly over the pale sand round their halted vehicles. Having done this drill, they tended to feel safe and virtuous. There was clearly a big task ahead.

As my part in the preparation of this manual I was given the subject of 'Shadow' to deal with, mainly using photographs to point the lessons. From the air, particularly from aerial photograph interpretations, the recognition of an object is possible more from the shadow it casts than from its actual top outline. I searched for really indicative objects and photographed them from above – from the balcony of the Continental Hotel – first in a flat light and

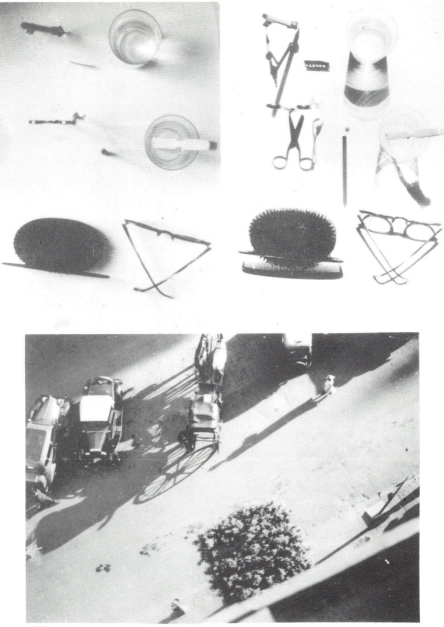

Tell tale shadows

then with a sharp side cast shadow.

On 24 March all the new Camouflage Pool Officers were taken on a flight over a large part of the Canal Zone of Egypt. We started at 7 am and flew over Abassayia along the Suez road and landed at Ismalia. The flight was very cold and soon I felt ill, was sick somewhere near Port Said, and felt foul till we landed at 12.15 pm. Disgraced! To have succumbed to air sickness on such a mild flight and under the very noses of one's colleagues was a real personal disaster and quite hard to live down. No one else seemed to be suffering. This trip was to let us get a bird's eye view of the area, the military and industrial targets standing out blatantly.

Shortly after this I reported to my new boss in camouflage, Capt Patrick E. Phillips (known as Pep), who was stationed with the Palestine HQ in the King David Hotel. I was to work with him and be based in Haifa. He was a professional painter – mainly, I believe, in watercolours – and after the war was head of the Byam Shaw School of Art. He sported a whispy military moustache and looked a very dapper officer, particularly for an artist. I went with him to Haifa on 3 April – the country very green and lovely, with lots of flowers and rich with the scent of orange blossom.

The military situation in Palestine at this time needs some comment. The Vichy Government in Occupied France could hardly be trusted to prevent the Nazis from preparing an attack from the north, through Syria or the Lebanon, and a defence programme was under way in the northern zones fronting these countries. There was also camouflage work to be done on anti-aircraft and coastal defences, mainly around Haifa.

When I look back on my period in Palestine I still feel a sense of frustration and wasted opportunity – that I did not absorb more of the rich quality of the land and its history. Admittedly I was historically rather ignorant, with no clear cut idea of all that had happened in this area throughout recorded history. The Christian places – Jerusalem and Nazareth, for example – became so familiar as part of my daily journeyings that the impact was lost. I remember passing through Cana for the first time and an unremarkable Arab village it seemed; there was never time to stop and consider and examine. More recent history, Crusader and Turkish, the Allenby Campaign of 1914-18, right up to the period of the Troubles preceding the war and still continuing, all gave the terrain an exciting atmosphere. Looking back it seems that I must have passed through it all in a trance.

On 10 April I went with Capt Phillips to visit Fortress One and the new Anti-Aircraft sites. The one I remember most clearly was on Mount Carmel, on the seaward end, with wonderful views westwards to the Mediterranean and northwards, up the gently curving coastline towards Acre and beyond to the Lebanon.

My task was to oversee and advise on the concealment and/or disguise of the many existing pill boxes. In the Azzib area north of

Acre (near Ras Naquora, the Lebanese frontier) the defence works extended from the flat coastal strip up into the rocky hills. The Cavalry division was stationed in a pre-war barracks at Azzib and part of their duty was to police the Teggert Fence, a barbed wire obstacle extending across north-eastern Palestine bordering Syria – named after a police chief of the period and constructed to help keep out Arab terrorists. The Cavalry, who must have been some of the very last mounted troops in the British Army, included the North Somerset Yeomanry, the Cheshire Yeomanry, and the Yorkshire Dragoons. I was also invovled with camouflage problems for the defence of the port of Haifa and surrounding district.

The oil pipeline from Iraq ended at Haifa, and there was a large and very vulnerable Tank Farm just to the north, run by the Iraq Petroleum Company. I had to try to arrange some camouflage there in co-operation with the civilians. We did our best, but the concealment problem was insuperable; the only measure possible was to make the draught board layout a little less obvious by disruptive painting and texturing – which might make a bomb aimer's task less simple if the light was poor.

April in Palestine is the very best time, when citrus blossom and lush wild flowers are in great profusion. These soon wilt in the heat of summer, but I was lucky enough to catch the full beauty of the Palestinian spring which I tried to record in watercolours.

The road out of Tiberias, westwards over the hills to the coast, passes the Horns of Hattim – a bare inhospitable shoulder of land where Saladin routed the Crusaders. The place seemed to retain an atmosphere of sinister doom. I very nearly met my own doom here. From Mount Carmel into Haifa the road led down at a very steep gradient and suddenly turned sharp left above a precipitous gorge. It had been raining after a long dry spell and the road surface was like ice. My driver started down too fast for the conditions and, realising this, he tried to brake. The truck went into a long relentless skid, and when it came to the sharp corner with the gorge below it pitched over the narrow verge. I braced myself for the plunge, then suddenly the vehicle bumped heavily, slewed round and skidded back on to the road. It continued to slither between the steep rocky cutting and the precipice, finally coming to rest against the cliff wall, where its wheels ran into the ditch.

While waiting for a recovery vehicle I went back to the skid corner to discover what had saved us. The tyre tracks on the verge were clear. Two ran straight off right up to the edge; another pair, those of the rear wheels, would clearly have followed except for the fact that one wheel had run into a square stone bollard. This had pivoted the vehicle round.

Another vivid memory is of the day when the Brigadier of 5 Cavalry Brigade whisked me off in his staff car to inspect certain stretches of the unfinished strategic east and west road. This hugged the Lebanese frontier and he felt that it should be screened to prevent the Vichy French and Nazis from observing British troops and transport movements. We were soon in the hills, steep and rocky in places and considered bad tank country. Having reconnoitred these stretches of the road the Brigadier left me and sped on eastward to Safad. My new vehicle and new RASC Driver Russell had been ordered to follow and pick me up, and I was left in a desolate spot by a bridge spanning a mountain stream. Almost at once it started to rain heavily.

After about an hour, with no sign of Russell and my vehicle, I walked back along the earth track, and soon realised what had delayed him. The road, merely a track bulldozed into the sides of the steep hills, was awash and walking was difficult. Eventually I came to a little hut by the roadside and decided to shelter from the torrential downpour. Inside I found a young Arab boy, who greeted me cheerfully but spoke little English. After we had sat in silence for a while he suddenly asked 'How is the enemy?' and tapped his wrist – not asking how the war was progressing, but simply the time of day! He then brewed up some thick and very sweet Turkish coffee, which he served to me in a tiny cup.

Soon after this a Jewish motorcyclist arrived and agreed to give me a lift – which seemed a good offer but resulted in one of the most scary rides of my life. The man had some object on the back of the bike and I had to sit on the handlebars. In spite of the slippery surface, steep descents and hairpin bends edged by precipitous drops, he made no effort to hold back his speed. Maybe he knew that, in this kind of driving, to brake could be fatal. But we survived and I found Russell, rather a lugubrious character, sitting forlornly in the truck.

My brother, John, had been stationed in various corners of Palestine with the police before the outbreak of war. The old city in Jerusalem must have been the worst station, where bomb outrages were common, and I recall a rather grisly incident which he recounted on his return. After one explosion the police had to collect whatever human remains they could find for possible identification. A severed forearm and hand had to be kept overnight for finger print identification and, as the station refrigerator was out of action, it was left outside on the windowsill.

Native Arab labour on north Palestine defence line. Syria in background and Bedouin tents.

When John went to recover it in the morning he opened the upstairs window and disturbed a cat settling down to devour the lucky find and resolutely determined not to lose the prize. It made off, dragging the arm across the flat roofs.

By the early days of May the main front line defences were well in hand and it was necessary to start on the second (reserve) line. This consisted of tank ditches and more concrete pill boxes and command posts. The work was done by Jewish contractors with Arab labour, overseen by Royal Engineers, but a close watch had to be kept to make sure the contractors used both a correct concrete mix and correct procedure for pouring. There was one bitter scene when a man was caught using a weak mix in order to make the work quicker and more profitable. When threatened with dismissal he pleaded for his family and children. It did not seem to occur to him that if the Palestine defences were bodged the Nazis might more easily catch up with him and his family.

Some of the work was in banana plantations and olive groves and here one came very close to the whole nature of the country and its people – the complete contrast between the highly organised Jewish Kibbutz and the happy-go-lucky lifestyle of the Arabs. On the surface the relationship between the Jewish contractors and the Arab labour was relaxed in spite of the difference of temperament. The Arab women were employed on tank ditch excavation and they carried out the work in their slow but picturesque way, carrying the spoil out in buckets on their heads.

One day, beside a track in the hills, I came upon the ruins of the Crusader castle 'Montfort', and it left a deep impression on me.

View along tank ditch from pill box

Here was this beautiful medieval building, recognisably intact but forgotten and isolated on a promontory in these remote wooded hills – its purpose lost and the drama of its days long forgotten. And here were we, contriving new defences, widely scattered and much less beautiful. These must be equally obsolete today.

To save travelling I decided to find a billet in the area and drove into the Jewish settlement of Nahariya. I rang the bell of a bungalow named 'Hause Pause', and a child peeped out. He shouted, 'ein Englander', then Frau Pause opened the door and I was shown a little room with metal mosquito gauze over the windows. We agreed a price and after a hard day I fell asleep, secure in the protection of the screens. But there were holes in them, and I was woken by hordes of mosquitoes. I put up my own fly net but the damage was done, and I had dozens of bites. At Nahariya there is a small brook flowing into the sea and this was the source of the multitudes of mosquitoes.

From Ras an Naquora to the Lebanese frontier the coast road going north climbed steeply up a cliff-like bluff, with the frontier posts at the top, and from the Lebanese side there was an extensive view of the whole Azzib area. The danger was that the camouflage superstructure disguising the pill box top or the loophole could become dislodged by shelling and fall over the loophole. The camouflage design had to be altered to avoid this hazard.

On 9 May my diary records, 'Meet Oldham, Ramsay, Goller and Fladr.' Oldham and Ramsay were Subalterns in the troop from No 2 Squadron, which was working in the Azzib area. Goller and Fladr were two regular Czech Army engineers. Varchek Fladr had escaped to Russia when the Germans took Czechoslovakia, was imprisoned, but later allowed to join the Allies. He was a cheerful and carefree young man struggling to learn English and already speaking quite well – with characteristic Slav intonation and some charming faults. One day I was looking at his English/Bohemian dictionary and said it looked good. 'Yes, it is very useless', he replied. Teddy Goller was an older, more serious character. I spent some very happy times with these two Czechs. They taught me (phonetically) what they considered to be basic and essential Czech:

Dobray eatow – Good day.
Dobray vetcha – Good evening.
Vee estay krasna – You are beautiful.
Eastay vee dobra divka? – Are you a good girl?
Day me hubishku – Give me a kiss.

These phrases have stuck in my memory through the years but have not proved very useful.

I have often wondered about my two cheerful Czech friends and what their subsequent experiences may have been in the difficult times in Czechoslovakia.

25 May was the day I met Col Collette and the Free French. This tough little French Cavalry Colonel had a considerable reputation for his exploits in Syria with his Arab troopers. They rode into the Yorkshire Dragoons camp unheralded and caused a great commotion. The Yeomanry, with their fine English Cavalry horses, seemed disdainful of the small, but tough and wiry, French colonial troops and their mounts, and were not at all cordial towards their new allies. One could not help wondering which type of cavalry would be better suited to the conditions.

The next day I took the road north from Rosh Pina, Tiberias, to Lake Hula (Golan Heights area) for a meeting at the frontier bridge with the Engineer-in-Chief and the Commander, Royal Engineers. The purpose was a tour of camouflaged defences – not entirely successful, the sun having moved round and revealed failings in the deception. In some of our disguises the concrete mass of the pill box was successfully absorbed into the rocky hillside by fake boulders, etc, laid over its smooth, rounded outline, but it was nevertheless given away when the sun, at certain angles and from behind, tended to throw up the real mass of the concrete shape. However, the visit seemed to go well. Barkas' visit from GHQ followed, but he could be relied upon to be appreciative of any achievement and difficulties overcome.

On the night of 7-8 June, at 2 am, the British and Free French attack on Syria and Lebanon (in which the Australians were involved) commenced, but we knew little of it apart from removing road blocks. And on 10 June an event took place of little concern to the world in general but of great importance to me – my eldest son, Simon, was born. The actual day of his birth passed without excitement, for it was several weeks before the news reached me.

At this time I was able to arrange a few observation flights over the defence areas to check their effect from the air, and was also promised a flight in a Blenheim over the operational area in Syria and Lebanon. The plan miscarried, and later I heard that the Squadron who went on the flight were intercepted by the very effective French fighters and mostly shot down.

Shortly after this I made an official visit to Sidon. I had no business to go beyond Ras en Naqoura but it was exciting to be up at the top of Naqoura, looking down on all the familiar defence areas. The coast road northwards hugs the sea shore, passing strings of little bays closed in by cliffs, whereas the Palestine coast is flat, with sandhills.

Approaching Sidon, where the front line was reported to be, I was on a stretch of road open to the sea when quite suddenly a small warship appeared, flying an exaggeratedly large tricolour and sailing parallel to the road. Before the full implication had dawned on me I saw flashes on the ship, heard the sound of gunfire, and felt a series of explosions burst on and around the road ahead. I took cover in an olive grove and, after watching the French ship proceeding unchallenged up the coast and out of sight, I drove on to Sidon. This was only just short of the front line but the citizens were carrying on normally, doing good trade selling odds and ends to the Australians who were in occupation. I went to a little café on a terrace overlooking the harbour and watched artillery in action to the north. Everything seemed abnormally peaceful until a fierce burst of rifle fire broke out below the terrace. Suspecting a sudden French counter-attack everyone rushed to the side of the terrace and looked down, only to see a group of Aussies shooting fish in the harbour below.

The 22 June entry in my diary records, briefly and undramatically, 'Germany invades Russia'. But in Palestine (while Hitler emulated Napoleon's greatest mistake) camouflage activities continued as usual, and I remember laying out 18 pill boxes in one day in the plain of Esdraelon (part of the second line of defence). Laying out a pill box involved finding positions which were tactically satisfactory and at the same time offered some opportunity for concealment or disguise. It was unusual and a good new development, for a camouflage adviser to be consulted *before* the defences were made, but great speed was required in order that the work was not delayed. 18 pill boxes in one day durnig the hottest season was quite a performance.

When visiting one of the sites near Jenin, after excavation had been started, I noticed among the spoil a number of irridescent glass fragments with some recognisable broken glass vessels. They turned out to be Roman, and after the war I described these finds to Professor Garstang, one of my father's patients who was a great authority on the archaeology of the Holy Land. He pressed me for exact locations and, as I still had my military maps, I was able to supply them.

Life in Palestine was not all pill boxes and disguise, and on 7 September I and Lt Silvester (who had joined me as 2nd Lieutenant and was known as Silvo) decided to give a party. The

INVITATION

to Mrs. Siegel

SYKES AND SILVESTER
HAVE PLEASURE IN INVITING YOU TO A
MOON LIGHT PARTY
TO BE HELD AT 8:30 O'CLOCK - SUNDAY 7th SEPT. 1941.
PLEASE FIND YOUR WAY BY THE ABOVE DRAWING
AND SOUNDS OF REVELRY ∽ c/o KOWALSKI - HAUS SPIELVOGEL - TOP FLOOR

owner of the apartment where we were billeted, Mr Kowalski, agreed to the use of his flat, and Naomi his Jewish maid and other Jewish friends offered to help with the catering. We invited guests from all our various contacts – services and civilians, and also Jews and Arabs, which was rather unusual and perhaps asking for trouble. A small band from a Sapper unit agreed to play for us. The flat, being on the top floor, gave us the chance to use the roof as an extra open air space, and there was a full moon that night, the weather balmy and fine. We spent lavishly on refreshment and this roof-top party was remembered with pleasure long afterwards – most of all by the local guests of both factions who had mingled without friction.

On 19 September I learned that I had been appointed GSO2 Camouflage to the newly-formed Eighth Army, which meant promotion to Major, and I reached Jerusalem five days later. At this important point in my war career, however, I went down with fever and was admitted to the 60th General Hospital in Jerusalem. From my ward window I looked out on a section of the old city walls, and in the evening I heard the boom of the Ramadan gun when the Mohammedan Fast ended.

Among my companions in the hospital were cavalrymen of the Scots Greys. Even at this period of the war cavalry units, both Regular and Yeomanry, were still not mechanised, with the exception of the 11th Hussars and 21 Lancers, who had been equipped with tanks and armoured cars in the 1930s. They had become the crack troops of the Desert Rats. The Scots Greys, on the other hand, were only now being converted, and the many casualties of this regiment who I met in the 60th General Hospital in Jerusalem were all victims of cuts and abrasions, broken arms, and so on, sustained in their efforts to come to practical grips with the business of armoured vehicles. The sight of these eager young cavalry officers poring over manuals about the intricacies of the petrol engine was, I suppose, symptomatic of our state of unreadiness to cope with Rommel's Panzers and Blitzkrieg.

By 4 October I had recovered and was back in Cairo. My diary says, 'Six months since last in Cairo. Same smells.'

4

My new posting as General Staff Officer Grade 2 (Major) at the HQ of the recently formed Eighth Army, which now took over the command from Western Desert Force, represented rapid promotion. The appointment of a G2 Camouflage to an Army formation had not been made before.

On arrival in Cairo, however, I fell ill with the same fever symptoms as in Jerusalem (among them rigors – sudden uncontrollable shivering fits) and I spent another fortnight in hospital, this time in the Fifteenth General, situated on the banks of the Nile. I read quite a lot and had more ENT treatment – rather grisly puncturing and washing out of the antrum in the cheek, via the nose. The local anaesthetic was administered by inserting a sharp stick, rather like an hors d'oevres stick, a long way up my nose. I recall sitting waiting in the passage outside the operating theatre with this long stick stuck in my face and feeling rather foolish. Eventually I was discharged and, after a few days in Cairo discussing the new job and being briefed by Col Barkas, I spent a short period on leave in Alexandria before setting off on the desert road to join the Eighth Army.

I arrived at the Eighth Army HQ at Sidi Bagush on 25 October, driving up from Alexandria in about seven hours. Sidi Bagush was one of the prepared defensive positions known as 'Boxes', created during the period of the Italian advance on Alexandria and Cairo, which had been turned into a total defeat by the Western Desert Force under FM Wavell and Gen O'Connor. It was sited between the road to Mersa Matruh and the sea coast and consisted of elaborate underground HQ offices connected by subterranean tunnels.

The Headquarters personnel lived above ground in tents and the Mess marquees were also above ground. When I moved into my predecessor's tent I was treated to a delightfully lurid female nude, painted on the underside of the tent canvas, which floated menacingly above my camp bed. I believe the camouflage brethren left many such traces of frustrated talent as they moved about the desert. Another 'artist camoufleur', Felix Harbord – a top interior designer in peacetime – was posted to Tobruk during the siege and found time there to paint a complete *trompe l'oeil* period interior in one of the few reasonably intact houses.

At Eighth Army I was to work largely under the direction of the G1 (SD) (Staff Duties) Col David Belchem. I had been well prepared for a cool and unsympathetic reception from the regular and senior staff officers under whom I would have to operate, but this did not prove to be the case with Col Belchem. However he was overworked and liable to forget my existence, so I busied myself for a day or two settling in, visiting stores depots and workshops, and contacting the various people on whom I would have to depend for information, stores and labour.

Two days after my arrival I was suddenly sent for by Belchem and told that an important conference had already started – which I should be attending. This was in the office of the AQMG (Quartermaster General) Brig Robertson, and the heads of the numerous services (Royal Artillery, Royal Army Service Corps (Supplies) REME Ordnance, Royal Engineers, Royal Army Medical Corps) were all there.

The subject of this conference was the nearly completed Desert Railhead at Misheifa, which was to play an essential role in the supply of the impending operation Crusader. Misheifa was situated some 70 miles to the west of Matruh, the old railhead of the desert line from the Delta, and 30 miles due south of Sidi Barrani.

I hurried off through subterranean tunnels in search of the conference, and eventually located the door leading to the AQMG's office, behind which voices could be heard. Through a narrow crack in the door I could see a lighted interior and a flash of red tabs which I guessed belonged to Brig Robertson. However, people were leaning against the door and their shifting about obliterated my view sporadically. I hesitated to batter on the door to be allowed in and, late as I was, to face the stare of the Brigadier and all assembled – then, peering through another crack, I saw that there was a second door in the wall opposite, unimpeded by standing figures. I threaded my way round to this door, opened it as noiselessly as I could and shuffled inside.

At this point the Brigadier was systematically pointing at each member of the assembly, going clockwise from one to the other and demanding: 'Gunners – any questions? Sappers – OK? Medical – any problems?' and so on, all the way round the room. When he came to me he stopped. 'And who the hell are you?' he asked. 'Camouflage, Sir' I replied. Then, sweeping his hand in a wide circle to encompass a layout plan of the huge complex railhead at Misheifa, he said: 'How are you going to hide this lot then?'

Although I had not yet had a chance to visit the railhead I knew that any idea of hiding it was ridiculous. Finding my voice at last, I said: 'The only thing I can suggest, Sir, is to make a decoy railhead.' He was clearly somewhat taken with the idea, said he would put me in touch with the Railway Construction Engineers, and I was to come back and see him afterwards. The pointing finger moved mercifully on its way and soon the conference broke up.

By 6 November I had had a full discussion with Col Anderson, who commanded the New Zealand Railway Construction Company. He was friendly and helpful in the decoy plan, his positive attitude to camouflage deriving from his memory of some effective work he had seen in Flanders during the 1914-18 War. He told me how at some point the front line had run through a brickyard and there had been huge stacks of bricks among the trenches. A machine-gun emplacement had been formed in one – by tunnelling through to the enemy side where a metal shield, painted to imitate the brick face, had been inserted during the night and the Vickers MG mounted effectively. It is strange to reflect now how remote and distant Col Anderson's recollections of the 1914-18 War had then seemed to me. Here am I, in 1990, recalling things already over twice as long ago, which yet seem to me fresh and recent. Col Anderson's memory of that First World War camouflage was the door to all the good co-operation he gave.

My plan for the decoy railhead, known as Depot 2, aimed at achieving two things. By appearing to be a prolongation of the railway work, it would persaude the enemy that we were not yet ready to attack; and by making it represent a tank delivery spur it would be of outstanding tactical interest to enemy intelligence, since the state of armoured strength and delivery facilities were of vital importance.

The extension of the line would have to be convincing. It was a great help, therefore, when Col Anderson proposed that, as there was a good stock of rails left over, he would continue to make the necessary earth formation westwards (beyond the Misheifa railhead, the nine miles we felt necessary) and the loose rails could then be laid normally – with the considerable difference, however, that sleepers could not be provided. But as the real sleepers would have had sand spread over them to help stabilise them and thus showing only partially, this drawback could be discounted. The first necessity was to fly over the completed track to discover what characteristic features should be imitated.

What could we hope to offer to the enemy air reconnaissance at the end of the nine miles of false line? Obviously we would have to construct everything we wished them to see – locomotives, box trucks, tank delivery trucks, tanks, dumps, AA defences, installation buildings, tracks – in fact, all the associated features which a glance at the real railhead (the size of a large village) would reveal.

To help me on the camouflage side I had, first and foremost, John Baker, who had come with me from the Delta. He was a trained Sapper Lieutenant, an architect pre war, with an easy and unflappable temperament, very hard working and good company. Life would have been impossible without such support. Between us we had to keep an office manned at Army HQ while we moved around in all directions – following up contacts with the subsidiary formations XXX and X111 Corps, foraging for materials, supervising the details of dummy construction, producing do-it-yourself instruction sheets for the making of mass-produced dummy tanks and so on. If John Baker did not express criticism of so ambitious and fanciful a scheme, I felt we had a good chance of bringing it off.

At X111 Corps, further forward, were Bainbridge Copnall, Philip Cornish and Fred Pusey, looking after the camouflage side. XXX Corps, with most of the armoured units, was served by Robert Medley. But my immediate concern was with the local means of creating the railhead props. Sgt Roff and Cpl Allison at Sidi Haneish RE Dump were at once involved in this, but the main

8th Army Steven Sykes and John Baker

source of hope in getting results in time was the arrival in the desert of what must have been the first purpose-devised Camouflage Unit – the South African 85th Camouflage Company. This special unit was a real boon and arrived just in time to make the decoy scheme possible. The detachments were officered by SA whites, the NCOs were whites and the troops were Cape Coloureds (of mixed white and coloured ancestry). They were well equipped with mobile power tools, but had no previous experience of the difficulties we faced in the desert, where it was impossible to acquire materials on the spot and requirements had to be organised from base.

Maj Von Berg commanded the 85th Company but at this point he remained in Cairo. His Second-in-Command was Capt Simpson, but it was the detachment Lieutenants that I came to know and rely on. At first they showed a healthy reserve about the decoy railhead project, but slowly, as it became hard fact and they began to see results, I sensed great support, comradeship and job satisfaction in their attitude. Two days after arrival they were making dummy train experiments.

I had the job of censoring letters from the 85th Company other ranks to their families in South Africa, and was surprised one day to read, 'As I write this to you, within sound of the enemy . . .' Then I realised that the sound came from the Prisoner-of-War cage sited alongside the 85th Camp.

The Cape Coloured boys had a very catchy anthem which they would chant as they worked on some monotonous task. The first three lines of each verse were repeated on rising notes:

> Hitler look out for the Camouflage,
> Hitler look out for the Camouflage,
> Hitler look out for the Camouflage,
> For the Camouflage boys are heah.

> Keep up the spirit of the 85
> Keep up the spirit of the 85,
> Keep up the spirit of the 85,
> For the 85 boys are heah.

Box Trucks were main rolling stock we had to simulate, and because of their size (some 15-20 ft tall) the most difficult. It was necessary to have a basic framework strong enough to sustain the canvas-covered box against sand storms. There was only a limited supply of hardwood of suitable length, and this had to be sawn up lengthwise, mostly by hand, to provide sufficient for our minimal

44

Depot 2. Views of dummy trains, transport and figures, also a dump of unserviceable petrol for decoy fire

Depot 2. View of dummy train

needs. An army cookhouse stove was converted to burn 'black' and produce smoke for the locomotive, and this was our prize creation. We had, however, come to the conclusion that there simply would not be enough material to construct dummies full-scale and so, while recognising the obvious risk of aerial photographs revealing the wrong scale, we had to take a chance. So the extension track had to be reduced very gradually in width to two-thirds of the correct size and all the dummies were scaled down accordingly.

My friends in Eighth Army Air Interpretation were full of foreboding, as indeed I was myself, knowing the incisive skill of the enemy's stereo viewing, careful measurement and comparison. I am surprised no one suggested that we set about recruiting a company of dwarfs to populate the decoy site. Dummy Bofors (light Ack Ack) were available for airfield protection. There was trouble when the Chief Engineer spotted a signal from a camouflage source ordering 300 Bofors – which should have read 30 Dummy Bofors. Abandoned unserviceable vehicles known as derelicts, of which there was a considerable and increasing number, were used in spite of their real scale to bulk up the effect of busy occupation. They were shifted constantly to new positions.

By the middle of November the NGP (Net Gun Pits) were

available as a quick and economical answer to the call for dummy Bofors AA gun positions. On 16 November my diary reads, 'Packing train, dummy figures. Work very late (BGS office move).' The Brigadier's move indicated the imminence of D Day for operation Crusader.

The next day I set out for Army Battle HQ (an abbreviated form of HQ used during operations, well forward of the main HQ at Sidi Bagush). I intended to reach the camp of 85 Camouflage Company which was sited conveniently near the decoy railhead site, but I had only got as far as the main railhead, and set out on the remaining few miles westward to find Lt Allen's camp, when the light failed. My driver and I had to settle where we stopped, sleeping one under the tailboard and one inside the vehicle.

The weather broke that night and there was violent thunder and torrential rain, adding to the feeling of drama and discomfort. By morning we were chilled and soaked, but daylight disclosed that the nearest camp, half a mile away, was Allen's. We were welcomed with mugs of coffee, served steaming hot by cheerfully grinning Cape Coloured 'boys'. I cherish many such South African welcomes. The storm had calamitous effects on the course of the

Depot 2. View of dummy train and figures

Depot 2

Rail extended
from Misheifa
9 miles to decoy
railhead

Dummy tank
made of
Gerida
hurdling and
canvas

Dummy lorry

48

Completed
tank

Mk1
Timber box
car frames

Mk2 Box car
frames

Depot 2. Mark II box trucks of metal rods

operations, but both sides were affected about equally.

18 November. Diary note, 'D Day. Landing ground 110. Sand storm.' I remember this water-logged landing ground and the anxiety over inability to fly the vital sorties. A sandstorm sounds impossible if all the sand is rain soaked, but it happened.

Punjabis provided labour for the NZ Railway Engineers, and I well recall watching while the whole rhythmic process of track forming with bulldozers, rail laying and fixing went slowly past me. The Indians, when handling the heavy lengths of rail, had a curious refrain-like set of orders which grew louder as they approached and dimmer as they moved on and away. It was all rather weird and dreamlike, but they left a very tangible metal track behind.

We issued information sheets on how all types of tanks could be quickly modelled in gerida, a cheap and plentiful native hurdling made from palm fronds. It came in sheets (about 2 × 1 metres) and was the standby material for dummy construction. The shape of the tank was covered with canvas and a thickly garnished net, causing it to cast a good shadow from which it would be hard for enemy intelligence to spot the 'hollow deception'.

There always remained the problem of the tank tracks, but as most of ours were supposed to have just rolled down the tank delivery ramp, this was not a serious problem. Tanks were normally carried on transporters right up to their start positions. Very soon Punjabis were allocated to the Unit, so we then had some live bodies on the site, and Maj Hall, of 27th LAA, was able to give us a minimum ration of two Bofors (light AA guns).

During the next three days my diary was blank but I have, even after so long, a very vivid memory of the missing events. I had moved my own tent away from Allen's camp to a point alongside the track, between the real railhead and the decoy. The country there was flat and only slightly broken by shallow ghôts. These ghôts were low-lying areas where the moisture tended to remain long enough for a tough scrub and other sparse vegetation to persist through the long dry season. Normally tents were put in these ghots rather than in the bare desert. In such a place I now camped with my driver.

At dusk, on one of those blank days, enemy aircraft started circling the railhead and then, as I watched and listened, they flew off westwards towards the decoy, passing over our tent. Full of anticipation I jumped into the truck and drove towards the decoy. It was now too dark to pick out anything clearly. The previous day the two real (as opposed to decoy) Bofors AA guns had taken up dug-in positions on the perimeter, and a small Sapper unit had been posted for work on the main feature of the decoy – a system of decoy fires, using a supply of unserviceable petrol laid out, together with combustible salvage, in a pattern of dumps; these could be set off singly or combined from a concealed control post in the centre of the site.

I was hoping to find this control post and join the Sapper Officer who had been left in charge. He had instructions to act realistically by firing the dump, according to the positions of the hoped-for fall of bombs, and with as rational a time interval as possible. When I thought we were in the decoy area I stopped the truck and jumped out. The sound of the enemy aircraft was much louder and lower now, and almost at once the tone of the engines indicated that a bombing run was starting. A stick of bombs straddled the site some quarter of a mile from where I was standing. In the silence following the explosions I waited expectantly to see decoy fires burst into flames. No such thing. I began to shout into the night, 'Let your fires go. For God's sake do something'. Still nothing. Then, just as I was about to move towards the craters, the entire pattern of decoy fires burst into flame.

The disappointment was great, for clearly the whole deception could have been revealed. Nevertheless, I was exultant at the evidence that our efforts had been proved worthwhile. No direct hits had been made but the craters were there for all to see. On my next visit to the G(SD) office at Army HQ the news had spread and I was received with some noticeable respect.

Towards the end of November Rommel made his headlong raid into the rear of the Eighth Army. This, we were told, would bring him straight to the HQ if he did not stop or turn off. He did turn off, and eventually the raid ended without disastrous results for us. But there were some very confused situations, scarifying confrontations and narrow escapes. Fred Pusey, for example, who was out on some task with X111 Corps HQ, found himself driving parallel with a column of mixed vehicles, and only after a time did he discover that they were German. He drove smartly away into the desert.

At this point I acquired a Morris Pick-up which proved a long term answer to my recurring vehicle problem. It was indefatigable and seemed immune to spring trouble, the main enemy in the bad desert terrain. I frequently drove in and out of slit trenches in it – but in the end it gave in. One day as I was driving across a stretch of good desert, I noticed that the vehicle seemed to be gathering and losing speed of its own accord in an alarming and unaccountable way. Later I was in the passenger seat and noticed a strange gap in the chassis which was opening and shutting. Without damaging a spring, we had succeeded in severing the main chassis. This was welded together in a few minutes by the New Zealand Railway people, and the old Morris PU went battling on. It was later named 'Kittyork' after my recently-married driver York's wife, Kitty.

1 December was marked by the capture of an enemy map showing the nine-mile extension of the railway to Depot 2. This was a relief to me, for I had feared the deception had been blown by the slip-up with the decoy fires, if not from the scale discrepancy. Evidently all was well. Instead we had another worry about a give-away of a different nature. At the genuine railhead at Misheifa a sudden night air raid had caught a row of box trucks loaded with German prisoners. Humanely, but possibly unwisely, they had been released from the lethal situation of being 'offered up' in boxes to the bombs, and some had promptly disappeared in the confusion. If they made their way west along the railway line towards their own lines they would probably have noticed the deficiencies in the track (no sleepers!) or the strange looking dummies at Depot 2. On the other hand we hoped they would have been so eager to keep to the open spaces that the secret might hold.

Rommel had now withdrawn from Tobruk, leaving the Halfaya, Bardia and Sollum garrisons. I spent some time with 13 Corps, with Fred Pusey, searching for jettisoned sunshields. These devices were light covers placed over tanks to disguise them as trucks from the air – sunshields being cast adrift when the units were ordered into action. Our aim was to recover them for further use. We also reconnoitred the area around the Omar strongpoints, Sidi Omar and Omar Nuovo. These had been constructed by the Italians as part of the Libya/Egypt frontier defences.

It was enthralling to be able to study their defensive system from the inside, built with some eye to comfort and well supplied with colourful Fascist propaganda material – the glories of the African Empire and vilification of Britain. Omar Nuovo was utterly deserted when I visited it, and as I went from one silent position to another in the chilly dusk, I was aware of a strangely creepy atmosphere – as if I were under surveillance by the erstwhile defenders. Later I was relieved to meet someone – in fact, Capt Byres of 2 SA Div, who kindly invited me to supper and lent me a bivouac.

In the changing situation it was necessary to allocate new tasks to some of the Camouflage Officers, and during this period Philip Cornish and I moved up to visit the New Zealand Brigade occupying the Meducar and Lachem area near Capuzzo. There was useful work to be done there with the 22, 23 and 28 NZ Battalions, and Cornish remained with them. From the elevated position here we could look back eastwards over the edge of Sollum barracks into Sollum Bay and the Halfaya Pass. We had a quiet lunch in the winter sun and watched the distant movements of Germans in the Halfaya Pass defences way below.

On the way back I met Brig Kisch, the Chief Engineer of the Eighth Army, to whom I had reported on 25 October. Then he had been civil rather than friendly. Now my diary was able to record, 'Congratulations from Brig on Railhead Decoy.' Brig Kisch was, I believe, Jewish and had a house in Palestine which had been attacked by the Arabs during the pre-war troubles. He was a regular Sapper of the British Army, with a very distinguished reputation.

The following day (7 December 1941) while back at Army HQ, I heard the news of Pearl Harbour. It all seemed remote and even (to us) unimportant compared with our own local war effort; but overall it was a great relief to know that now the Yanks were finally involved. On the 8th we heard that a snap daylight raid had dropped bombs on the middle of the dummy dumps – a welcome proof that the decoy was still working and, moreover, still deceiving in daylight.

Geoffrey Barkas, in his book *The Camouflage Story* (published in 1952) describes us at Eighth Army: 'They thought of nothing but dummies. In the daily log book, where all events were noted, one entry ran: "15.25 hrs. Depot 2 flown over at 5000 ft by three dummy aircraft!"' He gives the date of the first raid on Depot 2 as 28 November and credits us with nine bombs; he was incorrect, however, to say that 'Sykes pressed the electric buttons for the decoy fires.' But the effect was the same. A little later on he refers to the railhead as being at Capuzzo, but we were, in fact, miles short of Capuzzo, which was still in enemy hands. The actual spot was Misheifa – the kind of nowhere in the open desert which suddenly became a major target. He also stated 'more than 100 bombs were dropped on the dummies' – perhaps more than I would have claimed myself.

We had good publicity at Army HQ and as a result I tried to acquire a vehicle for the new Mobile Deception Squad which I was hoping to form. Of course all Army units have to be backed up by an official establishment, ie a clear-cut approved strength in men and equipment, and normally it would have taken many months to get a new unit approved. The desert was probably the only place where such special units could hope to sprout and flourish. In due course we were able to establish our unit, specially conceived and equipped to be able to produce the maximum visible demonstration of false activity by decoys, fires and explosions.

On 16 December my diary reads, 'On to Tobruk. Meet Cornish, Pusey and Galligan.' Edwin Galligan, an exhibition designer in peacetime, had been in Tobruk during the latter part of the siege, having taken over from Peter Proud, who found himself shut in Tobruk when Rommel's first advance cut off the 'fortress'. The many ingenious schemes Peter was able to contrive during the worst months of Tobruk's siege are all well described in Geoffrey Barkas' book, *The Camouflage Story*.

Two days later I was sent for by the BGS (Brigadier General Staff), firstly to be congratulated on the result of Depot 2, and secondly to instruct me to plan a decoy port installation to try to draw some enemy attention from Tobruk (possibly Bengazi also, when operating). The whole effect of these long desert advances was nullified by the extensive supply line immediately created. To supply Tobruk entirely by sea would obviously be beneficial in defending what we now had and in proceeding towards Tripoli later. It was an entirely new experience for a Camouflage Officer to be consulted in this way and I felt, as at the underground conference, very much on the spot.

I embarked at once on a scheme for the decoy port installation and in a couple of days was able to submit a plan to Col Belchem, who agreed in principle. At the same time he agreed to our vehicle for the Mobile Squad. This was a captured German Ford 3-tonner and had been a workshop lorry, fitted out with elaborate shelving and lockers – ideal for our purpose. As the nucleus of the unit I already had Lt David Jeffreys, who had come into camouflage in the desert via the operations in East Africa. He was a Lieutenant in the West African Rifles and had been tea planting when war started.

I had tried to meet him by flying from Sidi Bagush to Siwa Oasis where, as part of Crusader, he was engaged in camouflage duties with Oasis Force, preparing to advance far to the south, across real Sahara conditions, to Giarabub Oasis as part of Crusader. On that occasion my driver and vehicle showed up too late to get to the airfield, and I only met David Jeffreys after Crusader, when Oasis Force was disbanded and he was available for a new posting. He seemed ideally suited to run this new and unconventional unit. In addition authority was obtained for Medley to visit the forward transit camp and pick out the most suitable team available. The newcomers were mostly cheerful Cockneys from the Rifle Brigade.

SUBJECT:- Success of Dummy Railhead Scheme.

ADV.HQ. EIGHTH ARMY, MEF.

HQ/8A/S/140/G.

18 Dec.41.

G 11 (Cam).

1. Will you please convey to all those concerned in the construction and maintenance of the Dummy RH my congratulatio on the success which the scheme has achieved. The very considerable organisation, labour, and artistry employed in the No.2 Depot Scheme have proved well worth while and the results achieved are a very excellent reward.

2. I would like a report in greatest detail with photograph of No.2 Depot including a diary of enemy action against it prepared by you, so that the scheme can be tried again in other places in the future.

Lt-Gen.
G.O.C-in-C., EIGHTH ARMY.

TGJ.

Copy to Lieut-Col.Anderson, Railway Construction Engineer, N.Z.E.

Neil Richie Lt Gen GOC-in-C Eighth Army

56

Col Belchem had not only agreed to my outline plan but he had also given it the code name Belsea. Briefly it sounded simple enough. We were to distract attention from Tobruk by appearing to be developing some other port with a high priority function such as delivering tanks, fuel and ammunition, as at Depot 2. It seemed that all we had to do was to find a plausible location along the coast, westwards between Tobruk and Benghazi. The next essential was to get naval advice and help in reconnoitring for such a place.

I received a signal on 23 December from Adv HQ to see the SNOIS (Senior Naval Officer In-Shore Squadron) regarding the Belsea project. After the visit Lt Cdr Harris, Royal South African Navy, was appointed as Liaison Officer, and drawings for the scheme were started. Harris was a friendly and cheerful man. I thought he resembled T. E. Lawrence and we got on well.

On Christmas Day I went with Harris to Gazzala area in search of a site for the Belsea project. Our Christmas lunch, for which we had saved our best rations, included tinned Christmas pudding, which we ate with a good soaking of whisky from the NAAFI, and thus fortified I decided it was a good moment to practise with my revolver. Harris had one too, so we pitched the empty whisky bottle out to sea and took turns trying to hit it – which neither of us managed to do. I felt very happy and carefree (drunk!).

Reconnaissance continued further westward, Harris having charts from which places with suitable depths could be investigated. But still nothing satisfactory was discovered. So Harris, Pusey and I, with our drivers, continued westwards into the Jebel AKhdar (green hills) area of North Cyrenaica. This was a wonderful change after the previous endless stretches of sand and bare rocky formations. It was the area Mussolini had tried to colonise with Italian peasant families, and we came through centres such as Giovanni Berta and D'Annunzio, with the white colonists' villas and one or two more elaborate colonial buildings and churches.

We turned north from Giovanni Berta and soon passed the lovely ruins of Cyrene, then over some wooded hills into sight of the distant Mediterranean. The light was fading and on the twisting and precipitous road bridges and culverts had been partially demolished. So we decided to stop and spend the night in an empty Italian café. We were in very good spirits and had managed to improve our rations from an abandoned Italian dump. Nevertheless, as the wind rose and heavy rain fell, we began to consider the possibility of interference from pockets of Germans or Italians left behind in the recent advance. This could easily happen when troops were cut off, between the desert push to the south and the coastal advance.

We took turns at guard duty through the night, and I remember the creepy feeling of the deserted building, with the wind rattling damaged windows and doors. In the morning we carried on down the last stretches of winding road, and eventually reached Ras Al Hilal. This Ras (headland) was the most northerly point of Cyrenaica, and had been developed by the Fascists as a show disembarkation place for the Italian colonist families. The hinterland was green and interesting with tree-covered hills enclosing a fine sheltered bay – a heartening, if untypical, introduction to Africa for homesick Italians. A fine curving road and tunnel led down through the rocky hill to a small beach enclosed by steep cliffs.

There was a substantial concrete jetty, which had been partially demolished at the landward end, but there were no port installations of any size. The tunnel, too, had been partially demolished, so presumably the Italians had considered the place might be used by us for landing war material. In the flat hinterland Il Duce's architects had devised an impressive communal centre in the Islamic style – a mosque, shops, administrative offices and open-arched arcading which surrounded a rectangular piazza. Altogether it looked more like a film set than an authentic North African habitat. At any rate our search was ended, and we drove back to report that Belsea had found a home.

No 1 Deception Unit Ras Al Hilal

58

The jetty at Ras Al Hilal

5

1 January 1942. We spent the night in a colonist's home between Maddalena and D'Annunzio and were up before light. There was no rain at first but it soon started, was very cold, and we were soaked to the skin by the time we reached Cyrene. Here the ruins and well preserved mosaic were fascinating. We pushed on in very stormy weather, not helped by my vehicle being short of hood and windscreen, but we reached Bomba Hut by about 4 pm where we spent the night; then we continued to Advance Army HQ where I saw Col Belchem and later Col Barkas. There were useful discussions and good signs that the camouflage people were getting together for the new Belsea venture at Ras Hilal.

3 January was cheered by the arrival of two aerographs from Jean (dated 30 September and 13 November). My new Driver York (Rifle Brigade) reported, and I went to see the Deception Unit at the camp near the POW cage. All seemed in excellent order, and our German 3-tonner was packed with explosives. I then returned to Bomba Hut, after an unpleasant drive, still having no screen or hood and the clutch of the Morris refusing to come up of its own accord. I devised a method of pulling it up with a strap, but this had to be phased exactly with the driver who was working the gear. The road was narrow and full of tank transporters, and the whole journey, in black-out conditions, was nerve racking. I had bad rheumatic cramp in my shoulder and fell ill, probably with a temperature. Four miles from Bomba Hut we had a puncture.

By the next day another attack of fever was threatening, but I had a fairly easy morning and drove to Derna with Cornish, Pusey and Jeffreys with his lads. We took the coast road and decided to spend the night in an ex-Italian Air Force hut, all eating together and taking considerable trouble over the concoction of a prune, cream and whisky pudding.

That night has lingered clearly in my memory. We were in good spirits and everyone became cheerfully busy with the evening meal, making a warm fire and organising odd unusual little comforts for our stay, such as a table and chairs. Some of the real characters of the desert campaign were the drivers, generally taciturn men, not too ambitious but long suffering and given to rare and sometimes very telling utterances. On an occasion like this they came out of their shells. I recall a memorable rendering of *The Barley Mow* from Driver Coleman, and some very funny anecdotes from Driver Trow who told, in a broad Birmingham accent, of his pre-war adventures as a milkman. He treated us to stories of episodes with amorous themes and also confessed, almost with disbelief at his own audacity, that he had been engaged to two young ladies at once.

Trow was a master of understatement. One day, when he had been driving me along an almost impossible boulder-strewn track for an hour or so, he turned to me and said solemnly, 'This road's very bumpy'. Driver York could remain silent for long periods. There was one occasion, when he was driving me during a withdrawal and our spirits were particulary low. We were making speedy progress by desert standards yet a horde of flies continually encompassed us, and breaking a long silence I commented 'How the hell can these bloody flies keep up with us?' York considered for a long time and replied, 'Oh them . . . They've no sense of gravity.' After a typical quick desert lunch of bully and biscuit, swallowed in about two minutes dead, he would comment, 'Well, that's me scoff, I've had it.'

That evening in the Italian Air Force hut was pleasantly memorable in spite of the fact that I was feeling rough and feverish.

'First year from home today' I wrote in my diary on 5 January. 'Bad night with fever or something. Leave about 8.15 am along coast road.'

We had considerable difficulty at various wadis where rain had destroyed the track, and at one point there was a 50 ft gap in the road. The clutch and brake jammed together and I had to use the strap, as before, to pull the clutch up. The road, hugging the coast, on the map looked an easy straight drive from Derna to Ras Hilal – it was actually part of the Via Balbia, Mussolini's triumphal way to Alexandria. However this stretch had presumably never been finished as far as bridges and culverts were concerned, so it was cut up badly wherever the winter rains sent heavy torrents down to the sea.

For a few days I moved around between the Army HQs and the Belsea site (now re-named Belsey Bill by us). I had a longer look at Cyrene and the abandoned Italian and German dumps. One contained some very colourful but lethal-looking German shells for anti-tank use. They slimmed in a series of stages to the nose and the final projectile was very slender and sharp. They were colour coded in bright rings of paint. If a sculptor could have packed as much atmosphere of threat and contrived a form so lethal in appearance as this, it could justifiably have been hailed as a work of expressive genius. I kept one of each type in my truck – to my great regret and embarrassment later.

David Jeffreys was at Ras Hilal with his mobile squad and the German 3-tonner – sinister because of its alien black colour and the stock of explosives lurking within. It was now even more sinister because, on the way through Derna, they had picked up a human skull and fixed it on the radiator.

On 15 January I went to Benghazi to sort out a XIII Corps signal. Bainbridge Copnall, at XIII Corps, was liable to send very melodramatic signals. One at the outset of the Crusader operation had caused critical comment at Army HQ and I had been asked to explain it. It read, 'Battle joined. All camouflage officers in action.' One could picture our camouflage people chasing madly after the enemy and catching them in camouflage nets like butterflies.

This time Copnall had signalled demanding all the available detachments of the 85 Camouflage Company. My diary records, 'Decide send only Jeffreys.' This indicates that I had resisted his demand.

It was exciting to be in Benghazi, the biggest town since Alexandria, but by 18 January I was back at Belsea. The plan at Belsea was to:

a Appear to have repaired the demolished jetty (called a Dolphin by the Naval people).

b Make and float some moveable dummy ships.

c Produce some plausible installations (oil tanks) and signs of activity on the clifftop above the tunnel.

d Suggest that the partly demolished tunnel had been repaired.

e Show a concentration of tanks, etc which had been landed.

Newdigate and Allen, with their 85 Camouflage Company detachments were at work on a and c. Allen's first oil tank had just been erected. Newdigate's jetty work was up to schedule and a plan for a fake but floating ship was under way. I had a plan also for a ship superstructure (not actually floating) to be developed, which could be 'hung out' from the jetty. At least one enemy plane had circled the site and we were hopeful that already in these early stages enemy interest had been aroused. Plans were afoot for the Navy to provide, in addition, some real shipping activity.

The Poles from the Carpathian Brigade stationed near the main road offered available troops to seal off the area from chance or international snooping, but we discovered that, in spite of sealing off the road entrance in this way, long camel trains of Bedouin Arabs were continuing to file through the area, near enough for recognition of the fake work. I have a clear picture of Fred Pusey trying desperately to halt such a column and a delightful bilingual screaming match in progress. We managed, therefore, to have a detachment of the Libyan Arab Force for guard duties also. The result was a really international command: British, South African, Polish, Libyan Arab, plus a pioneer unit of blacks from Mauritius.

I again took refugse in the Bomba Hut, this time just with Driver York. The fever had eased, but I had a boil on my forearm of which the scars still remain.

The next day considerable lengths of steel wire were taken off Italian 'spiders'. This was for use in constructing the dummy craft. The real Bofors defence had arrived with Gunner Officer Lt Ainger. We had also acquired another memorable item – a *Loaf*. A loaf of bread was a rarity; biscuits had been all we had since leaving Alexandria.

By 23 January two oil tanks were complete and the dummy bridge span was up. On the 25 January the Mauritians were ferried to Derna by 85th Transport. I visited the Libyan Arab Force and discussed guards, then organised covering of the tracks by 85 Camouflage Company. Finally, feeling that everything was progressing well – and perhaps still fortified by the loaf – we decided that evening to have a party in the 85 Company billets.

This was an ill-fated party indeed. All was going well when there was a sharp rap on the door. I opened it and a figure, half hidden in the darkness outside, clicked his heels and, in a gutteral accent, asked, 'You Mayor Sikkis, ja?' For a moment I thought the Germans had caught up with us, then I realised that it was Lt Michaelovsky, one of the Polish soldiers. He handed me a signal. Its orders were to close down Belsea and move everyone back forthwith.

I knew that we were likely to be cut off on the main road if Rommel's sudden return had progressed as far as we feared, but although we moved off with speed, on the main Derna-Benghazi road there was a steady stream of communication transport moving eastwards and progress was difficult. Our spirits were very low as we travelled through that night, for it was clear to each of us that this was the end of all our preparations, plans and hopes for our promising Belsey Bill.

6

I returned to Army HQ through a dense sandstorm, and the note in my diary for 26 January is explicit: 'News scarce and general depression.'

A confusing and dispiriting period of some weeks followed, although Rommel's advance, which could well have penetrated further, was held up short of the old front at the outset of Crusader. Tobruk was not encircled, and the original decision to move all materials, from Depot 2 was not necessary. But our precious Deception Unit had disappeared. Rommel's advance had caught many units off balance, and our little band was just one of them. Philip Cornish had been left in charge while Copnall, Jeffreys and Sgt Roff had gone forward to Msus. Later they had driven to Belsea, hoping to join up with us, but found the place deserted. They had then tried to return to Giovanni Berta, up the steep mountain road. The truck, already giving trouble, had refused the climb and had to be abandoned. They rolled it off the road into a ravine, and made their way back as best they could.

I was at El Adem camp, where we had begun to collect our people to re-form. It was exposed, dusty and noisy from the nearby airfield, and I have no happy memories of it. Here, eventually, Copnall and Jeffreys turned up. In all this gloom we had, on 1 February, a desperate kind of party, playing drawing games which got ruder and ruder as we drank more and more captured Italian plonk. Medley, Copnall, Jeffreys and Baker were at this party.

On 2 February we obtained another captured truck for the Mobile Unit, but disquieting news came through about withdrawals, including that of the Advance Army HQ to Sofafi. However, I set out for Bardia to contact the Railway Construction Engineers. As usual there were sandstorms and a bad road, but I was able to discuss plans with our old friend, Col Anderson.

Another decoy railhead had been proposed, not by me this time but by the Staff at Army HQ. I felt it was a little unsubtle to repeat the ruse, but it was a sign that the long-term picture was not so black and that the desert railway was being pushed westwards from Misheifa. The route of the line was to cross the Egyptian-Lybian frontier due north of Fort Capuzzo.

My diary's 6 February entry is typical and confusing to interpret,

The Western Desert – cannibalized vehicle

Halfaya Pass

but nevertheless the essential flavour of desert life comes through: 'Advance HQ (which was a way back!) – Acroma, try cutting across NW of track but get involved in wadis. Sofafi, Buq Buq, Bardia, Gambut (petrol and lunch), Tobruk, Acroma, and seven miles west to XIII Corps. Rear HQ. See Camp Commandant, who directs me to Advance HQ XIII Corps, three miles 190 degree but unable to find it in dark. Bivvy. Have scrap meal, bully and biscuits, usual trouble with Lewis's primus stove.' Driver Lewis of the Long Range Desert Group had temporarily replaced York.

Next day: 'See BGS Brig Harding ref minefields and dummy columns. Leave 1.30. Get to Buq Buq and have to stop for dark. Most uncomfortable and cheerless meal – biscuits and Marmite. No tea. Primus bust. Getting a cold and feeling thoroughly miserable and tired.' And the next day: 'Buq Buq. Leave without breakfast. Spring gone on Ford PU – over 650 miles since 4 February on very bad surfaces.'

Early in February a Col Clark appeared – a very spruce, senior (and elderly) Staff Officer in an immaculate British camelhair coat. There was an air of mystery about him, and on the 9th I met him for discussions on Wireless Telegraphy for 37 Royal Tank Regiment – also details of Bedouin tent colours. Col Clark wielded deceptive power via wireless messages and agents, and it would seem that tanks of 437 RTR were to become Bedouin tents – a further sign that the deception side of desert camouflage was being taken seriously at HQ MEF. Two other regular officers arrived – to 'take over our camouflage efforts and put them on a professional basis.'

G1 Deception, Col Goff, and G2 Deception, Maj Gregson, arrived after having trouble finding the camp in the dark and landing in a ditch – setbacks noted in my diary with a detectable note of satisfaction. Nevertheless it was obvious, and recognised by us all, that the higher the level in the Staff hierarchy at which camouflage and deception could be represented, the better chance it would have of being planned effectively and tactically, and of linking it to the other hush-hush techniques of misdirection by W/T and agents which would greatly increase its effectiveness.

It is with some feeling of dismay that one learns later how planted information can be much more effectual on the one hand, and, even more, broken enemy codes on the other, as compared with all our scurrying about and decoy building on the ground. Because of 'Ultra' all the enemies' WT traffic was decoded, and such a disclosure makes much of the earlier discussion and arguments about values of generalship largely irrelevant.

Col Goff was a Regular in the King's Liverpool Regiment but

was not himself from the Liverpool area I was disappointed to learn. I had been happy to work under Col Belcham, who by now understood our value, capabilities and limitations very well. Col Goff, although amiable enough, was liable to emerge from Army conferences and announce that he had undertaken to lay on decoy work, the practical difficulties of which he had not grasped.

The site selected for the next decoy railhead (Depot 3) was at Point 207, marked Alam Abu Dihak on the map. I went there from Army HQ on 11 February. Col Anderson was reassuring about the new project, but this time he could not supply any rails – a bad blow, causing us to think of some substitute. The obvious alternative would have been timber, but there was none available.

There was only one material to hand in a sufficiently large quantity – thin tin plate. The British forces in the desert were supplied with petrol in what were known as non-returnable cans. 'Non arriveable' would have been a better description, for the gauge of the metal of these five gallon containers was too thin and the shape too badly designed (with practically no stabilising indentations) to stand up to being carried in three ton lorries on desert tracks and finally being roughly dumped. I remember trying to find a full containerr in a petrol dump and only succeeding after discarding several that were punctured and empty. The 'non-returnable' was also made of a very bright shiny tin plate and difficult to hide.

Despite their obvious failings these tins had become the universal answer to needs of all kinds in the desert. Split lengthwise they were used as In, Out and Pending trays in the HQ offices. Perforated at one end and filled with sand they became the filters by which washing water could be cleaned and re-used. At one of the desert track crossings (known as Piccadilly) there was a giant Eros figure made of tins soldered together.

It now occurred to me that if the cans were slit, opened up and flattened they could be hammered into shape over a length of railway line. Clipped together and painted black they would resemble rails. Other half-tins, split diagonally and also painted dark, could represent the protruding tips of sleepers as at Depot 2, and would look very realistic. There were drawbacks; a daunting number would be required and they would be vulnerable to damage. Fortunately Depot 3 was itself to be a spur, or complex of spurs branching off the side of the real line, so that there was no problem of a long nine mile approach line as at the original dummy railhead.

On this project I worked closely with Sam Butler of 85 South

African Camouflage Company, who had a camp in a salvage dump in the middle of Depot 2. The first time I visited him there I was astonished to see a large many-windowed habitation into which he invited me. It was really very spacious, made of the cabs of all kinds of trucks – bay windows by the score – the floor carpeted with salvaged material, and an atmosphere of civilisation quite stunning after tents and bivvies and trucks and desert beds. He had some typically happy looking 'boys' with delightful names like Tuesday, who seemed to offer a constant service of delicious hot coffee. Sam was indeed a very civilised man, and a visit to his desert dwelling was almost as good as going on leave. He asked me to get hammers for the rail beating and a stove to form the smoke for another locomotive. Sad to say I had no luck with hammers or mallets, but I did get a stove after considerable fuss.

That evening (15 February) we heard of the fall of Singapore, and listened to the Prime Minister's speech.

Depot 3 was to be on the very edge of the old frontier minefield, and this made the area dangerous to reconnoitre after dark; the barbed wire demarcation of the minefields was becoming invisible as pickets were knocked down or blown over and buried in drifting sand. My diary entry for 17 February reads, 'A long muddling day, visiting 38 Royal Tank Regiment, finding 56 sunshields, and arriving at X111 Corps Advance HQ late. Fuss over sprouts.' The final comment needs explanation. I had, some time earlier, been able to buy a tin of Brussels sprouts at the NAAFI and had hoarded it, awaiting a suitable opportunity to open this rare delicacy. As I had missed the Mess meal I was to be given a scratch supper, so I handed in my cherished tin of sprouts. But what I received was the usual meat and vegetable mash. I protested, and was assured by a rather hurt cook that he had indeed put the sprouts into the mixture. The horror of his incident is still with me!

On 19 February I saw the G2 Maj Carver, about the Depot 3 site, and this was agreed provisionally. (Maj Mike Carver is, at the time of writing, a Field Marshal and TV personality with views on nuclear defence much favoured by the anti-nuclear lobby.) The normal track formation had to be followed, ie earth moving by bulldozer to level out the track. This was possibly the most telling part of the game, as a bulldozer can make more recognisable tell-tale signatures in a given time than anything else. So this was the first move, and nothing could be done until it was finished. I decided that initially I should camp on the site to supervise work, and I sent for Sgt Roff and Cpl Allison as the most reliable partners in the task.

Roff and Allison arrived on the 25th in a bad sandstorm – visibility only a few yards – and we had a hard time pitching our tent with wind, sand and hard ground, but got it up eventually. I have happy memories of the time spent in that tent in the early stages of Depot 3, Sgt Roff, Cpl Allison and I. We had acquired an HMV portable gramophone and several records. The one we played over and over again was Bing Crosby singing *The folks who live on the hill*. The other side was *The pessimistic character with the crabapple face*. We liked this too, but I cannot remember the other records at all.

It was very cold at night so we had laid a double strip of hessian all round the bottom section of the tent. I had never forgotten the *Seven Pillars of Wisdom* description of how Lawrence slept in the cold of the desert with his followers, and each morning they had delicately shaken out all the snakes and scorpions that had nestled in for warmth during the night. We never attracted any snakes in this camp, but when we struck tent to move on there were several scorpions living in the hessian.

Track laying occupied the next few days, contending meanwhile with the dust storms. Roff and I spent the first morning correcting the geometry of the layout, put up the main crossing and I inspected progress on the rails (about 250), but another dust storm was starting. Later I heard that there had been bombs on Depot 2 and the camouflage materials set alight.

On 2 March, when work had ended and we were cooking our meal outside the tent in the fast fading light, we saw a truck heading straight for the minefield where the fence was down. We fired a round of tracer bullets across the front of the moving vehicle. It pulled up, and from it emerged a Maj Kidd, RA, and an Army Chaplain. The truck was from an AA unit moving out of Tobruk, where they had been stationed ever since coming to the Middle East. They had no idea that all the names spattered over the Western Desert signified physical features – for example, desolate Birs (wells), Sidi (graves of Islamic holy men and prophets), and Wadis (dry water courses), all with individual identities. These names never indicated a village – which they were hoping to find, with buildings in which to camp as they had done in Tobruk.

This episode was marked by a singular coincidence. Before the war I had corresponded with a Benedictine monk from Buckfast Abbey in Devon regarding his stained glass work – hoping, incidentally, to get a chance to work on the Abbey glazing. The Chaplain turned out to be this same Benedictine – Dom Charles Norris. They had a drink with us and we advised them about

Western Desert camping; then they left before it became too dark.

The desert seems to be the place for coincidences. Only a few weeks later two other examples came my way – chance meetings with two old school friends. First, I ran into Jackie O'Sullivan on 21 April, a regular soldier acting as Air Liaison Officer. In my last year at school (1932) we had played in the same rugby side (proudly unbeaten in school games) but I had not seen him since. His sister was the film star Maureen O'Sullivan, who went to Hollywood in the thirties; the actress Mia Farrow is her daughter.

The second reunion was about a week afterwards, when I was visiting armoured units and called at X Hussars camp to ask for directions to 2 Armoured Div HQ. The trooper I spoke to said, 'Maj Archer-Shee will know.' Then, to my great surprise, I came face to face with Bobby Archer-Shee, who was a special friend of my brother Michael. He had just come back from leave and reported some bombing in the vicinity of the Capuzzo area. This sounded as if it might well be Depot 3 doing its stuff – a guess which proved to be correct. Incidentally, *The Winslow Boy* story is about the Archer-Shee family.

To return to the early days of March and Depot 3; I was keeping a rather low profile following the arrival of Col Goff and Maj Gregson, but there was worse to come. Two more regular officers put in an appearance – Col MacNamara and Maj Innes (the latter complete with kilt and shepherd's crook). They were involved in intelligence or deception and wanted to be shown around. As usual there was the feeling that the regular officers regarded the camouflage artists as amateurs.

Rain is the memorable feature of 4 and 5 March (up to 1 ft deep in our tent, and books, bottles, etc floating) and work continued in torrential downpours. I got soaked through pitching Col MacNamara's tent in the early hours of the morning, but then managed to get a good deep sleep in my faithful bed roll – a ready-made bed with sleeping bag, sheet, blankets and pillow all carefully made up so that they could be rolled in the canvas valise, to be unrolled at a minute's notice. Wherever I was, however calamitous the latest situation report, come rain or sand storm, I could be sure of a good sleep. Preferably there would be a tent of some sort between the bed roll and the elements, but often enough the bed roll was all I had or needed. This was normally a prerogative of officers, but in the desert army regulations and practices had become eroded, and in our little camp we all made ourselves equally cosy. When I eventually returned to England and was billeted in a house with a bed, I still laid out my bed roll on it and instinctively got in. Throughout the war, except during such crises as the Calais episode or D Day, I managed to wear pyjamas every night.

Anyway, on this particular morning the first thing I became conscious of on waking was a bottle of VAT 69 moving slowly past, almost level with my eyes. I then realised that the tent was awash and the water level was about to reach Sgt Roff's hammock-like structure. Roused, he pulled his captured Italian trumpet out of the flood and blew a gurgling kind of reveille which woke Allison. Until now, our everyday problem was shortage of water, so this situation seemed ridiculous. In fact, this storm was more serious than we realised at the time, and had caught troops unawares who were camping in wadis which had been transformed in minutes into rushing torrents. Some men had been drowned.

Our immediate reaction was to think of some way of saving water before it disappeared as quickly as it had come. Plastic sheeting would have been a boon, but polythene had not yet arrived. So we filled every available container and then had a good bath in the flood. We were cut off for a day or two, our vehicles being well and truly bogged down, but our old friend Sam Butler came to our aid by sending one of his trucks over higher ground to within walking distance of our camp. He sent us a generous offering of South African rations and a delightful little quotation from *King Lear*:

> Poor naked wretches, wheresoe'er you are,
> That bide the pelting of this pitiless storm,
> How shall your houseless heads and unfed sides,
> Your loop'd and window'd raggedness, defend you
> From seasons such as these?

Depot 3. Flooding camp of 4-5 March 1942

Depot 3. Flooding camp of 4-5 March 1942

When the problems of the water and the Colonels had subsided life at Depot 3 continued as before, and on 14 March we moved our camp back to the Ghot. Efforts were being made to get a rooter (a machine for rooting up a furrow in the ground to lay water pipes or underground cables) for this was an important adjunct to any military position in the desert. We had decided to construct water towers to add to the deception picture, but all our problems were complicated by the high winds which followed the floods.

There was an especially bad dust storm on 21 March, three box cars being blown over in the high wind and we had to see that they were securely fettered. At Depot 2 a whole train blew away and we had to sent out search parties down wind to recover what we could. The locomotive, once it broke loose, rolled rapidly out of sight.

On 23 March I was summoned to the CRE's office at Army HQ. Col Edwards, the CRE, reminded me in appearance of the gentleman in a busby who used to grace the packets of Greys cigarettes. He evidently had received a recommendation for an award to the Sapper officer who had made such a muff of the decoy fires at Depot 2. From me he wanted confirmation that his officer had indeed been performing what, in the commendation, sounded like an act of sheer self-sacrifice in sitting dutifully in the centre of a target area. He was, in fact, securely dug in. It must be understood that when the time came for units to submit their award proposals, none would care to submit a nil return. I did not feel it my duty to enlighten Col Edwards of the full facts and I had not been asked to do so. I do not know if a medal was awarded but I am sure, if it was, that it was quite as meritorious as many another.

On the same day John Baker went on leave and I took Roff and Allison to Rear Army for money warrants and Matruh transit passes. And so the little camp came to an end, but this leave taking was lightened by the arrival of Col Barkas on one of his trips from GHQ. I always felt heartened and supported by his evident enthusiasm and relish for a chance to get into the field and away from the office atmosphere of Grey Pillars, the MEF HQ building in Cairo, peopled by what was cynically known as the Gaberdine Swine – a reference to their smart gaberdine uniforms.

Geoffrey Barkas was the force behind a quite unusually welcome collection of bumph which was sent to all outlying camouflage people – 'Camoufluers' as he called us. This publication was called *The Fortnightly Fluer* and had a serious and useful purpose in keeping us all up to date on developments and camouflage ideas and equipment. I recognise the talents of David Jeffreys, Brian Robb and Tony Ayrton in these offerings but some of the others, whose initials appear, I did not know.

Sadly, on my return from Mersa Matruh, I found that disaster had befallen Depot 3. On the night of the 24th a Brigade of New Zealanders, withdrawing from the front for a well earned rest (in darkness, during a bad sandstorm) had driven right across the site, ignoring the planned crossings which we had sited and signed to help convince enemy air interpreters of the genuine character of the place. This incursion, together with the sandstorm, had just about wiped out all our weeks of effort. I photographed the dismal scene of collapsed box cars, etc – the petrol tin lines were squashed out of shape and dispersed in all directions. It could, of course, be painstakingly restored, and it was.

Depot 3. Dummy railhead at Alam Abu Dihak after sandstorm

Pages from 'The Fortnightly Fluer' of April 1942

A MESSAGE TO "FLUERS".

In this war of lonely groups of scattered tents and
trucks it must be hard enough, even for the men of
a Battery or a Battalion, to capture and hold that
warming sense of belonging to a Corps or a Regiment
with a story, a tradition and a comradeship of its
own.

One might think it even harder for the still more
widely scattered "Camou-FLUERS" of the Middle East
to keep that feeling of community. And yet I think
we do. It was easy enough at first, for we were
very few. But we have grown a good bit in fifteen
months and it would not have been difficult to lose
our identities and that sense of "belonging"; because
there has not been much to belong to -- except the
job.

Therein, I think, lies the answer. For some reason
or other, the job demands - or does it create? - a
quite extraordinary enthusiasm, and a faith. There,
perhaps, is the comradeship of camouflage. We do
not seem to have lost it. It is profoundly to be
hoped we never shall.

That is why this publication is a Good Thing. It
is our Regimental Journal of the "Middle East Camouflage Corps". I believe it is to be called the
Monster Spring Offensive Number. No matter how
monstrous or offensive it may turn out to be I shall
still like it.

April, 1942.

- 2 -

Spring Offensive

Some of us Paper Warriors have decided to launch a Spring Offensive.

Four previous attacks were delivered in 1941, at fortnightly intervals, the main objective being to provide useful information.

This time we send you nothing useful. Light charges only.

"Take Post".
"CAPS on".
"Five words rapid.   FIRE".

CRUEL CLEVER CAT

Sally, having swallowed cheese,
Directs down holes the scented breeze,
Enticing thus with baited breath
Nice mice to an untimely death.

CAUTIOUS MINNIE

Sally's cruelty was great.
Minnie's guile was greater.
Declining the ethereal bait
She donned her Respirator.

FINALE

This tale in Minnie's litter
    Is passed from chin to chin,
How Sally's sweet yet bitter
    Breath had always failed to win,
Though helped by scents of Roquefort
    And Gloucester Double Blue,
The charms of Brie and Camembert,
    The strains of Port Salut.

- 4 -   G.T., A.M.A., G.B.S.H.

You will obs
A curious gr
To wit (to-w
The Goonah,
    The lesser

Their sense
The wonder i

Observe the Owl. Its plumage, see,
Grows lighter *UPWARDS* gradually,
Thus emphasising, undismayed,
TELL-TALE effects of light and shade.
    A pity is it not ?

The little G
(Or anywhere
Whatever hue
The place wh
    Or make a

Nor amongst shadowed stems to hide
Are Snots with stripes and spots supplied.
In Spotless Stripeless lands they dwell
And think that Stripes and spots look well,
    An emptyheaded lot.

these words
sts and birds,
tinking Owl,
juinea Fowl,
Snot.

age is small:
e at all.

The Fowl's as bad: a mimic true
He'll mimic me or even you
Or Captain Cott— or anyone
Not for protection but for *FUN* '
Which *I* think it is not.

ur room
assume
st
s up his post,
ot.

These creatures group with that strange brute
The Contra-Countershaded Newt.
Their origin is in dispute.
Some people think they constitute
Nature's reply to Cott.

On 1 April I had contacted the RAF about a recce flight and was shown 'a useful paper on camouflage' from the Air Ministry. The next day, when about to take off at Gambut, the airfield was attacked. I had been settled in my seat in the Lizzy (Lysander observation plane), battened down under the cockpit cover with my note pad ready on my knee – at last I was to have a much needed and delayed look at Depot 3 from the viewpoint that really mattered. The pilot had not yet taken his place in front of me and as I waited I suddenly became aware that everyone had disappeared. The next minute there was a terrific roar and I realised that an enemy plane had just passed over at a height of a few feet. I did not hear any shooting or bombing, and presently some ground staff appeared to help me out. The enemy air activity was considered too much to allow the flight.

I left on 4 April to go on leave and arrived at Alexandria just before dark. This leave was coupled with a trip to the Staff College at Haifa for a lecture which Col Barkas was anxious I should give outlining the new approach and techniques for camouflage and deception which we had been developing in the Western Desert. I dined at a small restaurant in Alexandria – French cuisine and wine served by a very dilapidated and aged French waiter in a worn, rather grubby waiter's evening dress and dicky.

To be eating alone on leave was a real anticlimax, and I think that, with no one to share my bottle of wine, I must have got rather drunk. I decided to give the old waiter a really handsome tip and told him not to be so miserable – all in a carefully prepared little speech in French. It all miscarried. He was so astonished and confused – for obviously he could not understand my speech and assumed that I was complaining and there must be some snag in accepting the tip. This was followed by a bad night in a room shared with a 'snoring wog' – not a lady wog I would add.

Next morning I and Driver Lewis drove to Cairo. He was a diminutive ex Long Range Desert Group veteran who had been loaned to me in place of Driver York. My welcome by the camouflage people in Cairo was very warm and enthusiastic, and I was made (very enjoyably) to feel something of a hero. My diary says, 'To Tommy's Bar for party with David Jeffreys, Brian Robb, Fred Pusey and others. On to the Russian Club. Pass out.' I wondered afterwards what the Russian Club was. No Russians seemed to be about, but there certainly was vodka – and that was what caused my downfall. I remember being put into a taxi, even being able to repeat my complicated Cairo boarding house address, being supported into a lift and through a hallway (where my companions helped themselves to a bowl of bananas) before being deposited in my room. Strange the details a vodka sodden brain can retain. I was really worried about the bananas.

The landlady, a French woman, brought me a large English breakfast in the morning, but I was deep under a violent hangover and could not face any of it. She told me that a soldier was waiting for me in his car outside and with horror I remembered what the day had in store for me. I had to get to the railway station, on to a train for a stiflingly hot 18-hour journey to Haifa, there to deliver my lecture to an assembly of top brass – highly intelligent, and no doubt critical, Staff Officers.

I asked my landlady to send the soldier up. It was Driver Lewis, and I offered him my breakfast, which he gladly disposed of. He had to try a number of times before getting me on to my feet, but at last I was dressed and we went down to the street. But the truck was not there and we looked at each other in horror. He, with his greater instinctive wisdom in such a situation, said 'It will be the Red Caps'. I had thought that the wogs had made off with my dear desert vehicle.

We took a taxi and toured the various Army Provost (police) Vehicle Pounds and eventually located our truck. The Provost Officer was coldly polite and said that it would be quite in order for me to remove it – after I had checked a list of objects he had removed from it and accepted his receipt for them as correct. The list was long and complicated, and it included all the German ammunition I had been carrying about since I picked it up in Cyrenaica, together with a motley collection of other objects – all of which were forbidden in the Cairo area. I had no time to worry about the chance of a Court Martial or whatever might result. I was now almost too late for the Haifa train, but I staggered aboard just as it was pulling out.

The 18-hour journey, in spite of being crowded and uncomfortable, at least gave me time to recover. The lecture seemed to go reasonably well, although I felt that the most enthusiastic listener was Geoffrey Barkas. I met some old friends, John Codner who had taken over my Haifa job and Fred Pusey who was en route for Baghdad. Suzi, my office cat at Peninsular Barracks, was well. I was invited to a meal with my old landlord, Mr Kowalski, and Naomi (now Mrs Kowalski).

After three days leave I repeated the 18-hour journey back to Cairo. The return trip with Lewis from Cairo to Army HQ ended abruptly – two miles from the end of our journey a front tyre burst, the car almost overturning in spite of the fact that we were only doing about 25 mph at the time. I had been away 12 days.

On 1 May I saw Col MacNamara about Depot 5, for yet another decoy railhead was being proposed. This time the real one would be at Belhamed, a few miles short of Tobruk, with Depot 5 acting as decoy adjacent to the east side of the perimeter. A 'two-faced locomotive' was also discussed. This was my idea to outwit low flying enemy fighter pilots who had been shooting up trains, firing accurately into the engine boiler area and putting them out of action for a considerable time, repairs being difficult and lengthy. The desert locomotive had to carry a lot of water and the tender was very long. It was suggested that if the tender could be disguised as the boiler and the boiler as the tender, and if the engine went in reverse to pull its load, there would be a good chance that an accurate machine-gun attack would damage the wrong end. Such were the fantasies of the eager camouflage officer. I do not remember this plan coming to anything.

About this time Col Goff left the scene and Col Mainwaring came into the story. The main Army HQ was now near Gambut, between the Tobruk road and the sea. Tents were dug in with a row or two of sandbags, forming a low wall so that during an air attack one could lie reasonably well protected below desert level. One day I returned to hear that a large black snake had been seen in the tent and had made its escape by disappearing in a gap in the sandbags. This gap happened to be on my side of the tent, alongside where I would lie in my camp bed. Short of dismantling the tent and removing the sandbags there was nothing to be done. I was assured that these large black snakes were not dangerous, and I had to make the best of it, but a fear which had been hanging over me from the very moment of my posting to the desert had now become reality.

Another hazard in this camp was the scorpions. I was sitting on the wooden box which comprised the latrines and put my hand down the side to where the bog roll (toilet paper) would be. Not feeling it, I glanced down to see where it could be, and noticed the tail end of a sizeable scorpion protruding through a gap in the woodwork a few inches from my naked posterior. A more agreeable member of the local fauna was a chamelon, sinister in aspect but harmless and very interesting. It lived in our tent for several days, catching flies for us and regarding us with its weird revolving eyes. Naturally, being camouflage officers, we tried – without noteworthy success – to watch it change colour and pattern according to its background.

The fifth Decoy Railhead project was now well advanced, and

Gnat Cove, Tobruk

Gnat Cove netted over

Tobruk Cove netted over

83

Steven Sykes and Newdigate

85 Cam Coy working on dummy lighter under netting

Dummy craft Tobruk Cove

Two dummy sterns of lighters

also the other camouflage work in which we were involved, coded The Kennels. The object of the latter was to cause confusion as to the use of the coves, Gnat and Benkura, in Tobruk Harbour. Newdigate and Johnstone of the 85 Camouflage Company were in control. It is strange to recall how calmly we went on with this work after the start of Rommel's offensive of 27 May. The diary records, 'Battle joined Bir Hacheim. 250 German tanks move east then north to Knightsbridge (21 PZ Division) and Duda (15 Division). Results of action not clear. 7 Armoured Division HQ dispersed. 4 Armoured Brigade take a knock. To 13 Railway Construction Company. See Maj Smith and welding Sergeants. Go on to Depot 5 and learn of El Duda shelling. Get 85 Camouflage Company and others into Tobruk perimeter (map reference 419, 427). Trouble with car. Return to Army. Bombing and machine-gunning of camp.'

The El Duda shelling was over the top of the escarpment, not far from the decoy site. I have always had an uncomfortable feeling that this section of the Tobruk perimeter minefield had been lifted to allow access at the very point which Rommel had planned to break in. His programme had been forestalled in the previous November – Crusader started a few days before he had planned his offensive.

The attempt to encircle Tobruk by penetrating eastwards to the coast, if successful, would have come very close to Army HQ. In the event this thrust was contained and a curious period of normality returned with the continuance of the deception work for a further fortnight, until 14 June. Although I spent much of this time at the Gambut Army HQ (where it should have been possible to keep in touch with the situation reports and flag-studded maps) I was continually unsure of the progress of the battle. My new G1 Deception kept me well deceived. One forgets how long some of these desert operations took to swing one way or the other.

By 28 May the news was better. We learned that El Adem was not threatened and 90 Light Division had withdrawn south. But my diary was silent on the struggle raging almost continuously for 14 days only a few miles to the south west. Instead, a series of entries such as, 'To Gnat Cove. See work. Toning satisfactory but straight unbroken edge at sea end. Very good and rapid work. 40,000 square feet erected overnight by Lt Johnstone's detachment. Cove bombed. Moonlight raid at 300 feet. Six of 11 braces cut.' We were working on a plan partially to net over a cove and show the sterns of dummy lighters projecting at certain times to attract bombing. This was a reversal of the original attempt to net over the cove and use it as a hideout for real ships. But the effect of these subtleties was not to be tested properly as the fall of Tobruk followed on 21 June.

On 2 June I had the pleasure of driving a captured German Ketterdraftwswagen back from 13 Corps to Army HQ. This was a strange, almost toylike tracked vehicle which had not been seen before, and it caused much amusement on the Tobruk road, crowded with reinforcements driving west, and it was well received by Col Belchem at Army HQ.

Four days later I went with the Chief Engineer and Copnall on an inspection tour to Gazala and north to the new Durham Light Infantry box. We were bombed by nine ME 109s which swooped over us at 50 ft – an incident which left us shaken and with a tendency to laugh hysterically. The impact of sheer sudden sound was petrifying; with planes flying low and very fast one was always liable to be taken completely by surprise. From this trip I got a clearer impression of the nature of the confused fighting in the area known as The Cauldron. There was no front or rear to the situation, and pockets of each side were intermingled. The German tank thrust had run dry of petrol and water and was facing a total defeat, but at the eleventh hour it was resusitated by a penetration of the front defensive area (held by 150 Brigade of 50 Division) whereupon supplies became possible once more. On this day the outcome of The Cauldron was still in the balance.

Captured German 'Ketterdraftwswagen'

87

There was at this time a plan to conceal lighters alongside the wrecks in the harbour. This was to be done by suitable netting over the lighter, close in on the shadow side of the wreck, with an extended display of dummy damaged superstructure jutting out and over the lighter. Air photographs of the wrecks had suggested that this might work, but it was largely a question of first distorting the apparent damage, for it was not possible to disguise a lighter merely as shadow or sea.

By 14 June it was at last becoming clear that the battle had gone badly, and the depressing experience of a long withdrawal was to follow. Although what we were giving up was almost totally empty desert, yet each former camp and stopping place held indefinable but strong nostalgic memories of times when things were going well and expectations were high. Now the full extent of our reversal could be measured. Another depressing and very worrying aspect of such a retreat was the near certainty that, however thoroughly we eradicated our dummy work, such fixed evidence as the false track could not be erased without exposing its false nature.

15 June. Diary note, 'Back to Maktila (15 miles east of Barrani). Very slow and crowded roads. Take coast road. Lunch – somehow get picnic spirit in spite of retreat. Very near old February camp site. Have good swim – much needed.'

16 June. 'Stay at camp. Nothing to be done and very little news. Situation vague but menacing.'

20 June. 'Tobruk attack starts. Early news of break in the perimeter. Later worse news, and little hope by night.'

21 June. 'Fall of Tobruk. News in morning. Very hot. Allen calls. Had not heard of Tobruk. Is badly shocked, having two brothers and six in-laws there in Transvaal Scottish.'

Poor Allen's shock was family and very personal, but everyone was stunned by the news and the fact that Tobruk, so long a bastion and symbol of successful resistance to the Axis, had collapsed so easily. Col Mainwaring, who had particular knowledge of the Tobruk defence system, had gone into the fortress just before it was cut off and was captured along with the 33,000 other prisoners.

By 23 June we were back at Sidi Bagush, where I had reported last October. Elements of camouflage units began to reassemble, but things were altogether chaotic. 24 June brought further uncertainty, indecision and unsuccessful attempts to get some guidance or instructions from the G1. Eventually some dispositions were made with the BGS (Brigadier General Staff) approval. 85 Camouflage Company were deployed in the Alamein line.

The HQ moved again by night to Dabaa, where I got a good tent site in low sandhills near the sea. I was hamstrung by the fact that Col Mainwaring had taken my vehicle, but Col Barkas joined us and took me to Alamein, where we tried to make sense of the chaos. Barkas ordered our camp back twice, first 1½ miles east out of the Alamein box perimeter, and again 15 to 20 miles further west. We did nightlong watches, and I remember the loneliness of the place – long stretches of sandy beach gradually becoming visible as the inevitable Egyptian sun rose.

Another memory of this time concerns the painter Hal Wolf, a Lieutenant but no soldier at heart. He was absent when Barkas ordered the mounting of guards and other precautions, and when Wolf reappeared and Barkas told him rather testily that he was supposed to be mounting guard, he asked in his dreamy way, 'Why? Is anyfink wong?' Rommel was almost at the gates of Alexandria but it had not occurred to Hal that there was 'anyfink wong'.

I spent a day reconnoitring the whole of the Alamein line, from the sea to the edge of the Quattara Depression. The New Zealand Division was in a strange plateau-like feature, almost a natural fortress, but the so-called line seemed in places to be fragmentary and incomplete. The only significant contribution to be made was to see Commanders and offer to provide a trained Camouflage Officer to advise where possible, and also to supply such ready-made devices as the 'net gun position' (NGP), now much more readily available as we were so near the base area. An NGP consisted of a large rectangular net, dressed with features simulating the air view of a gun position. When raised on posts held up by guy ropes it provided a rapid and convincing impression of a real artillery position.

For two weeks in July life went on much as before. Gradually some constructive help was given to the units manning the line, mainly basic help in concealment of positions. Rommel had by now arrived in full strength in front of the Alamein position and had tried unsuccessfully to break through. The arrival of Alexander and Montgomery was imminent. The British and Commonwealth forces, sitting right on top of their bases and receiving heavy reinforcements, were fast returning to their ascendancy over the Axis forces, who had to contend with many hundreds of miles of supply line and a very limited reinforcement.

I had been told by Barkas that he wished to withdraw me from the desert. Although I was worn out, I did not really want to go; but the last few weeks had not been much fun, having neither the remote Western Desert atmosphere nor the dreamed of alternative of the fleshpots of the Alexandria and Cairo areas. Besides, all the old faces were disappearing.

11 July. Diary reads, 'Brian (Robb) does a drawing in evening.' I have it still. It was a pen portrait, and I can remember now the combined sound of him humming and puffing and the rapid scratchy sound of the nib on the paper.

On 13 July I drove to the Camouflage Office at Maadi, outside Cairo, and the next day I had to return my faithful Morris Pick-up to the base depot. I asked nervously what would happen to it, and the Sergeant indicated a pile of scrap. Shocked, I protested that it was worthy of a better fate. He clearly thought I was mad.

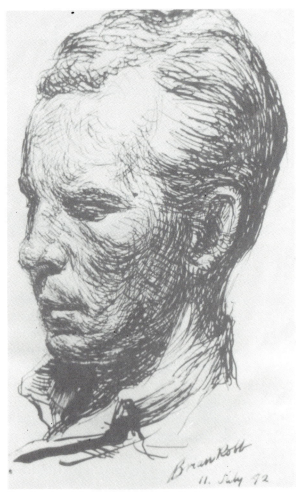

Pen drawing of Steven Sykes by Brian Robb

Driver York, Rifle Brigade and Steven Sykes in Morris pick-up Wadi Auda, Tobruk

7

Based in Cairo, I felt flat and curiously out of joint, with no sense of relief or pleasure in being out of the desert and living in some comfort, with rich and varied food. Col Barkas advised me to join the Maadi Club outside Cairo, and I did so, but I cannot remember making much use of my membership. At Maadi we watched cricket, in an atmosphere calm and untroubled by what was still a very shaky situation in the desert not so far away at Alamein. I became aware that two entirely contrasting ways of life existed for the Forces in the Middle East.

The desert situation led naturally to an easy-going attitude in military formalities – dress in particular. British Forces in Cairo, and particularly those at HQ, wore immaculate uniforms and worked hard at their many offices at Grey Pillars. I felt rather hurt that my old mates, who had left the desert before me, had already fallen into a life pattern where, at a reasonably early hour in the evening, they vanished to their digs around Cairo and to their private social routine.

Col Barkas asked me to write reports on the work we had been doing in the Western Desert, notably on the concealment of dumps and shipping, also other developments we had introduced at Eighth Army. He was at work on an ambitious and comprehensive Training Pamphlet. This appeared in October 1942 as *Middle East Training Pamphlet No 8, Part IV*, with the opening words: 'The purpose of these notes is to demonstrate the possibilities, the limitations and, above all, the requirements of camouflage, for the guidance of those Staff Officers who have had inadequate opportunities of studying the realities of the subject . . .'

This was a fairly polite way of telling the regular Staff that they needed more awareness and some real training in this department. His method was to pose a number of imaginary yet quite realistic military tasks which brought out all the essential thinking and procedure for their successful solution. These were:

Task 1. Concealment of a Forward Base.
Task 2. Concealment of an armoured Brigade.
Task 3. Camouflage protection of HQ against airborne attack.
Task 4. Creation of a 'Special' Dump (ie Dummy).
Task 5. Assembly of a 'Special' Brigade.

Western Desert. A typical scene. German minefield marked with pickets, non returnable petrol cans & exposed teller mine. Vehicles in heat haze.

Fort Cappuzzo, March '42. W (Viva) Duce & W ⑆ painted on gate posts of Nazi & Italian cemetery & a knocked out Matilda Tank.

The Tobruk road under repair with diverted traffic either side.

Convoy of troopships going past Combined Training Centre at Kabrit Point. Indian troops practising disembarking etc in foreground.

D-Day H + 190 minutes. Sword – Queen White beach. Tanks & troops moving to beach exit.

D-Day morning. Work on beach exit on Queen White.

Situation on Queen White shortly after landing, white beach marker & wind sock were removed as the German artillery ranged on them.

D-Day Dead. Queen White. Dead from both sides covered with tarpaulin.

D + 1 (Night). Queen White. Large landing ship discharging armour and beyond Rhino ferry discharging transport.

Sherman tanks knocked out in advance east of the Orne at Sannerville. (An in situ sketch.)

Road block on the Troarn road through Bois de Bavent held by 6th Airborne Division.

In situ sketch in Holland. This roundabout was made in an hour or so by demolition of houses.

4 Cdn Armd Div tanks at Rosmalen. Holland. Feb 1945

In situ sketch of Canadian tanks and locals in Rosmalen, Belgium during advance.

Blockhaus Sonja in Calais defences.

July '44. Operation Goodwood 'Oboe' – 1000 bomber raid.

The last task was, for reasons of security, not dealt with nor illustrated in the notes, but it was to be covered by a separate Most Secret Report which would be issued in the near future.

Much later, in June 1943, I emphasised in one of my lectures that most important of all was the change in attitude towards the desert as 'background' in which to exploit camouflage. From being regarded as a blank hopeless space, where all home training became meaningless and where good dispersal is the beginning and end of the matter, it came to be accepted as an ideal place for the building up of false pictures, the cunning substitution of real for false and vice versa.

Meanwhile, much progress had been made in the design and quantity of production of standard decoy equipment of all types, and the Camouflage Branch at GHQ had grown sufficiently robust and experienced to play its necessary part. The *Notes on Planning for Commanders and Staffs* (*METP No 8, Part IV, Operational Camouflage*), written and arranged from the foregoing experiences and published in the October before Alamein, now reads almost as a prophecy of the part camouflage played in that battle.

I was next sent by Barkas to HQ Persia and Iraq Force (Paiforce) in Baghdad on a kind of reconnaissance of the camouflage situation there. The day before leaving I again began to feel ill and wondered if I could go sick; instead I got rather drunk and had a very short night before boarding a flying boat on the Nile at 4 am. 'Take off 0500' I recorded. 'Feeling very feverish and ill. Saw crumpled brown paper mountains (Sinai) and then slept heavily. Altitude probably helped. Went ashore Kallia (Lake Tiberias) and was served lovely ice cold grapefruit juice by Safragis (Sudanese) in spotlessly white robes with red cummerbands and tarbushes. Habbaniyah Lake 1200 hours. Driven by Arab in very old saloon car over desert to Baghdad. Hotter with car widows open.'

The flight seemed to cure my fever. I visited the various camouflage people – Peter Proud at Tenth Army, and a very considerable and enterprising factory for making camouflage equipment – dummies, etc – run by Arthur Upfold. It was called Camspur and was sited beside the railway line. I visited Edwin Galligan in Basra (ex Tobruk Garrison in succession to Peter Proud). I then visited Abadan. The temperature in July was terrific all over Iraq, but the humidity in Basra was especially high and made the climate unendurable for long.

I returned to Cairo via Damascus on 12 August. This time I

travelled overland on the Nairn, a bus service started by some Australians after the First World War and still the only overland connection between Baghdad and the places across the desert to the west. The latest buses were huge, very powerful and beautifully sprung and roomy, but the main joy was that they were air conditioned. The journey across the desert tracks took 17½ hours.

Diary – 'Leave 1700 hours. Stop Ramadi for some tea just before dark. Sleep heavily. Arrive Damascus 10.30.' The sleep was the first I had managed for some nights. In Basra and Baghdad the heat, which had not abated after dark, had made sleep impossible although camp beds were on the rooftop. I returned to Cairo via Palestine by Staff car.

On 17 August I had to attend a Court of Enquiry concerning one of the subalterns in the 85 South African Camouflage Company. This was held at Helwan, near Cairo, and I recorded, 'Am first witness, examined for 3½ hours and badly bitten by bugs in wicker chair.' I can recall the horror of knowing I was being attacked by these insects but having to sit still.

I had a week's leave in Palestine on my way back to Baghdad to take up my new appointment of General Staff Officer Grade 2 at the Paiforce HQ, again travelling on the Nairn, which took 20 hours. Carl Wilton, the Camouflage Officer who had shared the cabin on the *Samaria*, was posted to Paiforce shortly afterwards and surprised us all by arriving in a small sports car – a Singer, I believe. He always liked to have a car of his own, just as he had during our brief stop in Durban.

There was no road, as such, leading eastwards out of Damascus – only a few sketchy desert tracks vanishing eastwards into the far distance. Wilton told us how he had driven round the eastern outskirts hoping to pick up a sign indicating Baghdad. No such thing. He began to arouse local Arab interest and a small group gathered. Pointing eastwards down a faintly discernible track, he enquired 'Baghdad?'. No reply. He feigned driving off, revving up and sounding his horn, and again asked, 'Baghdad?' This time an Arab got the message and, nodding his head, answered 'Baghdad'. Carl next tried 'Good road?' Again no reply. He then acted as if the car was pitching him violently up and down. 'No bumps?' he enquired. The same Arab again nodded and pronounced 'No bumps', whereupon Carl put his foot down and headed in an easterly direction. That he turned up safely in Baghdad never failed to astonish me. One evening shortly afterwards he left his Singer unattended in Baghdad – and later, inevitably, found it with all the wheels removed.

Tel: No: EXT:136.
G.H.Q. PAIFORCE.
500/6. G.(Cam.)

Dear *El B*.   7 Nov: 1942.

First of all,may we congratulate you all on
the truly terrific doings of the last fortnight.
You have no idea how this news has changed the
general atmosphere here, and believe me it needed it!
We are all thrilled and very hopeful,and those
of us who have "been there-and back!"before"are feeling not
a little homesick.
From your Personal letter BM/G(CAM).505 of 25 Oct
and from bits of news via Barclay,Hirst and others who knew of
the camouflage preparations I am as good as certain that   at
last we (Cam) have had our big chance to play the really
"Campaign Swaying" role,which we have believed in and fought
for so hard, during these last two years out in the M.E.
Newspaper reports state categorically that "Three
factors brought about the Axis downfall"-and first on the list
is their appreciation that the thrust wasto come in the
southern sector.
Unfortunately this is NOT sufficiently impressive
or reliable"ammunition" when one is out to impress Staffs.
(Remember the first communique of the November
Push last year.)
I was present in the Senior R.E. Mess- to which
Arthur and I have moved, when this recent mention of"Surprise
deciding a battle", was read.   I tried hard to direct their
Base-benumbed minds into grasping its full implication.
Believe me- they seemed neither impressed nor convinced,and one full colonel (Indian Service) gave his opinion
that it was all a toss-up,quoting Cambrai or somewhere from
the last war.   It will have to be rammed home far more
forcibly and officially than that!
Now what I am getting at is this.-
1.   You have already stated your intention of getting
         out a complete operational report on the show and send-
         ing it to PAIFORCE as"Lessons to the Commanders".
2.   This will neaessarily take time, what with the
         usual obstructions and your two outstanding Technical
         Reports to be done.
3   I feel that HERE the time is particularly ripe NOW
         for an attack on the Top Chaps- becaus e if we convince
         them now -they will have all this winter of intensive
         training to get used to this "new" weapon and include
         it in the War Games.
4.   The story,as from one Cam man to another,(even if
         incomplete in detail) could be used to great advantage
         to awaken interest in the critical sticky spots on Staff.
5   I therfore suggest that you send me the dope in such
         a way that it is freed of all normal limitations and delays
         for use as I feel best, but of course on the strict
         "Officers Only" level
6   This would help greatly to debunk the idea,still
         prevalent in this G.H.Q, that there is very little that
         G.Cam. need ever know on this elevated level. For instance
         I am not allowed in the War Room etc!
7   If this crosses your intentions I shall quite under-
         stand,& know that whatever success there has been will be
         exploitd to the full.
Please convey my personal congratulations,felicat-
ions and good luck wishes to Tony,Bryan,Summers,Cornish
and all the contra-countershade Desert Rats

                    Yours   *CBS*.

My time as G2 at Paiforce HQ was spent almost continuously in Baghdad, except for welcome visits to outlying units – the longest trip being to Teheran. When I was appointed to this HQ the importance of the Command was thought to be equal to that of Middle East Command, since the indications were that the German thrust towards the oil rich north of Iraq was likely to become a very real threat. Rommel's threat to Alexandria and the whole Egyptian delta area was at the same time causing all kinds of dire withdrawal plans down into the Sudan. Paiforce, therefore, was likely to become pincered by these two thrusts. It was, moreover, the only buffer to a drive by the Axis towards India. A large proportion of the troops in Paiforce were Indian.

Somewhat unexpected reinforcements arrived from the north when the Russians released a great many Poles who had fallen into their hands on the collapse of Poland. They were later formed into a formidable force under Gen Anders, but at this time they were merely encamped in Iran, organising themselves and enjoying their new-found freedom. One expression of their joy and pride was to lay out the shape of a huge Polish Eagle in painted rocks on the hillside beside the camp. This was not considered very good camouflage behaviour, but I beleive, in the circumstances, it was allowed to remain. If it survives the centuries it may one day prove a puzzle to archaeologists.

After Alamein and the end of the threat to the Delta, the threat from the north also receded following the Soviet successes, and soon Paiforce became more and more a backwater of the war. I knew instinctively that the twin aspects of camouflage would have played a significant part in the huge Alamein operation and felt very left out, for I had worked hard to create the right understanding in the General Staff at Eighth Army. At Paiforce the attitude of the General Staff to the camouflage people was clearly still that they were amateurs, and I was not even allowed to hear the inside news of the preparations for Alamein. Barkas had, however, done his best to keep me informed and to acknowledge my earlier struggles, witness the letter he sent me very shortly after Alamein:

Personal and Most Secret
BM/G (CAM) 1019

11 November '42

Maj S. B. Sykes, RE,
G2 (Camouflage) Paiforce.

My dear Sykes,
    I think it would please you to know that Camouflage was given a

96

very big job of work in the battle that opened on 23 October, that the job was done in the conditions that we have all striven for during the past 22 months, and that there is evidence that it was successful and repaid the considerable diversion of resources that were needed to carry it out.

˙I am writing a full and technical and operational report with pictures and statistics for future guidance, and this will come along officially as soon as I can get it finished. Meanwhile here is some advance information that may be interesting and helpful to you. It is Most Secret and very DO [demi-official] – but I see no reason why you should not show it to any very senior Staff Officers at your GHQ, particularly planning or operational ones, or even the C-in-C. I'm sure they would be interested. This however is at your discretion. Here is the general dope.

Camouflage appreciation and plan: We were taken right into the bosom of the operational family from the start. Early in September I was sent for by the DMO [Director of Military Operations] and then passed on to BGS of Eighth Army. I was told as much about the *Intention* as I needed to know and was asked to submit an Appreciation and general proposals. They told me about concentration areas and enough about scale, about periods involved, about axis tracks, about the main Cover Plan activities other than camouflage, and so on. I was asked what Camouflage could do and what it could not do – in short I was asked to produce a plan. You can imagine my delight. This was what we had all been working for. It was pie!

At first the Security aspect was so fierce that I was not allowed to discuss anything even with Ayrton [my successor at Eighth Army] but naturally he had to come in a few days later. But the general result was that I was able to lay down that while concealment of the *fact* of a concentration was impossible in this or that area, concealment of scale and state of completion was possible if certain things were arranged: that substitution of dummy formations for real was also possible, and concealment of final assembly might be done on certain conditions. You know the kind of appreciation I mean. It was also possible to decide, on what I had been told, that the most profitable thing was to concentrate everything possible on active deception – dummies in a big way, in fact.

Finally I was able to give a broad idea of the manpower, transport, real defence and other resources required to carry out the general plan in a given number of days.

Action taken by general staff: The BGS approved the Cam

Appreciation and Plan and turned the whole thing over to the BI (Planning) – Richardson – who amplified it a great deal to fit in with all the other major considerations, whether of the Real Plan or the Cover Plan, which he knew and I didn't. Within a few days Ayrton and I had been given a complete set of Camouflage Operational Tasks based on the agreed appreciation but now built in firmly with all the rest of the plan. We had a timetable, we knew just what we had to do and where it had to be done – and so we were able to crack on with manufacture and detailed arrangements of every kind.

Detailed demands for labour, MT [Motor Transport], liaison with Formations and Units, manufacture – all the rest came smoothly into place. It was heavy work – but what a pleasure it was. All these demands went through G(Plans) and were put through the proper Q or G channel and given their appropriate priority.

Outline of the camouflage operations: I cannot give you any details in this letter. It is enough to say that Ayrton ran by far the biggest and most varied part of the show well up forward – and we down here took over a big dummy scheme just behind. But you can judge the scale of the thing from the fact that in our piece of it alone we had to:

a   Make 400 'Grants' [American tanks] out in the desert.

b   Produce at least 1750 'MT' and many guns, etc etc.

c   Employ three complete Pioneer Companies, an entire General Transport Company RASC, the POW Unit *and* 85's Factory specially mobilised for the occasion, throughout the period of manufacture and the erection and maintenance of the show.

d   Employ a complete LAA Battery, Bofors, for defence while the scheme was standing.

Ayrton's jobs in the aggregate were bigger.

At Appendix A is the copy of a note I was asked to write for submission to the C-in-C. It gives you a fair idea of the nature and extent of the total Camouflage Operations.

Thanks to first-class direction and co-ordination by G(Plans) and to the fact that the whole job was put on a proper operational and executive footing right from the start all the schemes were done as per schedule.

Results: There is little concrete evidence to prove exactly what part of the admitted surprise was due to the programme of Visual Misinformation. There seldom is. But at all events the Army Commander seems to have been very pleased indeed. This can be said with certainty. The concealment of 25 pounder guns was proof against the air view and the enemy must have had the shock of their lives when the full barrage opened on them. And there can be little doubt that if the enemy recced the rear area of Eighth Army he must have thought that a whole Armed Division and an Armed Brigade, were still miles in rear when in fact they were up front. There are various other pointers – but I am studiously against making claims one cannot support with evidence. On the whole, however, we may be satisfied that the camouflage operations in their relation with the rest of the deceptive plan helped to fox the enemy in a big way.

More accurate information as to results is expected from 'I' sources and will come into my complete report which will come officially with a covering note from MO. So that is that for the time being.

I am also enclosing an advance copy of MET P No 8 (Part IV) *Operational Camouflage* – Notes for Commanders and Staffs, with the author's compliments. Besides which I also send a DO and Most Secret copy of a Report on Cam Nov 41 to 42. It sketches the growth of operational camouflage and the influences which have made it necessary – plus the obstacles that have held it back. It finishes at a particularly interesting pioint in relation to the job I have just described. You remember the howling failure that you and I suffered during the retreat to the Alamein Line. It is odd, and extremely satisfactory, to see how different the story has been this time. I don't see why you shouldn't show the report to any very senior officer on a DO basis.

I thought many times how you would have enjoyed handling this show seeing it was your struggles in the sand that did as much as anything to create the better conditions in which this job was done. Ayrton did outstandingly well. Never mind. It is nice to think that even if it never happens again there has been one big camouflage operation planned and carried out on sensible, economical and efficient lines, and it worked.

Forgive this long and rather effusive document. Maybe you will find it interesting. No doubt, now that there have been a few successful camouflage operations carried out, you are not having to 'sell' it as hard as you did in the difficult old days. I imagine, all the same, that you may not yet have all the resources needed for schemes on this scale. But that will come I expect, and despite the inspiriting events of the past ten days I don't suppose there's much danger of us running out of war for some little time to come.

Goodbye – and the best of luck.

Yours sincerely, (Sgd) G. de G. BARKAS

This communication from Barkas did a lot to dispel my rather disgruntled feelings at having missed out on the reward of my ten months' efforts in the Western Desert.

Very little of Baghdad was 'in bounds' to troops. David Jeffreys and I nevertheless spent some time dodging Military Police patrols and investigating the more colourful heart of Baghdad. There was a warren of narrow streets and one could soon get lost. David and I believed that somewhere there must be the enchanting Baghdad of the *Thousand and One Nights*. The reality always turned out to be much more sordid, but we did make some real Iraqi friends and were invited to their houses. I remember a very long evening sitting cross-legged on a carpet in the open court around which the houses were built, listening to interminable Arab ballad songs.

I was billeted in the Royal Engineers' Mess, which was an old Turkish house close to the bank of the Tigris. Although a Major I was the junior officer and found myself faced with the task of carving the joint at meals. Rations must have been good for us to have real meat to carve. I found the job formidable and by the time I was able to eat my own helping the rest of the Mess had long finished.

Again I went down with a very unpleasant attack of fever and was sent on New Year's Day 1943, to the 25 General Hospital on the outskirts of Baghdad. The hospital building was a huge old Victorian-type house, quite incongruous in a dusty stretch of dry desert. The Army had added corrugated tin and sacking latrines on the flat part of the roof. The ward I was in was very dark and crowded, and when I went for an ENT examination the strong light at once showed that I was a bright yellow colour.

I was pronounced a jaundice (or hepatitis) case and moved into another smaller ward, with just one other officer who shortly afterwards died of typhus. I used to make my visits to the latrines very early in the morning when all was quiet, with the dawn breaking. From the housetop I could watch the wonderful blue dome of a mosque at Khardimain slowly materialising out of the obscurity. In full daylight the scene was quite squalid, but the transformation at first light never lost its magic. When discharged I was feeling very low and was aggrieved at getting no sick leave. Worse still, and sending my spirits even lower, on returning to my Baghdad office I learned that my cat had been run over.

Towards the end of January I was involved in a strange deception exercise. A number of central European cabaret 'artistes' (suspecterd of pro-Axis sympathies) had been active in Teheran and had been expelled. They were to be sent back home by train, via North Iraq and Turkey. The scheme was to display a large number of armoured vehicles within sight of the railway line in the northern tip of Iraq, near the Turkish frontier. It could be assumed that such a significant concentration would be duly reported by the 'artistes' to Axis Intelligence.

I travelled up to Mosul, and from there made a preliminary reconnaissance with the officers from 62 Tank Regiment, whose troops were to operate the scheme. It took us some time to find a stretch of line suitably remote from villages and open enough for the dummy display not to be overlooked. The weather was severe – cold winds, sweeping rain and much hanging about with no shelter. We had settled on a place near the small village of Wailza. The dummy tanks and armoured cars had to be sent up from Camspur (the factory near Baghdad) and offloaded as secretly as possible to evade the prying eyes of the local Iraquis.

The packages themselves looked innocent enough – bundles of kits – the materials from which the vehicles would be assembled, but their distribution to the units working the various zones had to be discreet. The units then ghosted off with their packages and took up positions. None of the dummies was mobile – therefore a reasonable number of real vehicles had to be dispersed among them with orders to move about at the appropriate time. The fact that all stationary vehicles would be expected to be draped with camouflage nets was helpful as it allowed less detailed and less accurate dummies to pass muster.

The great day was 6 February and we boarded the train at Suburuja. The short period on the train was disappointing – no Wagon Lits service of luxurious refreshments such as we had hoped to find, and no sign of the glamourous 'artistes' we had been visualising. We heard later, for security reasons, an official on the train had insisted that the blinds be drawn. Perhaps this would only have had the effect of increasing the deportees' curiosity, and they would surely have managed a peep or two! But we never knew the success of this enterprise.

In April I again boarded the Nairn bus and then drove down from Damascus via Palestine. As I approached the Syrian-Palestine border I was surprised to see a frontier post manned, with the bar lowered across the road. I had no Pass as such, so I stopped a hundred yards short and wrote myself one! This satisfied the frontier officials.

13 April. My diary notes, 'Waiting for news of posting from Paiforce.' The exodus of Staff Officers from Baghdad left me with a sense of having been abandoned by the Camouflage people in

Cairo. Barkas had earlier indicated, in a long letter of advice, that my post at Paiforce should have been on a par with his own at MEF, ie a G1 with Colonel's rank. This had never happened, and I had not pushed for it in any way. What concerned me now was the feeling that the action was all moving back to Europe and that it was vital somehow to get myself posted to some formation which would be moving in that direction. Instead my posting, when it came through on 22 April, could not have been more depressing. I was to go for an indefinite time, to the Combined Training Centre in the Suez Canal area.

8

The Combined Training Centre (CTC) was situated at Kabrit – a promontory jutting out between the Great and Little Bitter Lakes which formed the southern end of the Suez Canal. The Centre was a permanent school for training formations and units who were to be used in amphibious operations.

I had hoped to be posted back to an operational appointment, ideally with the Eighth Army. By now, of course, the Battle of Alamein was long over and Montgomery had moved slowly and relentlessly along the coast, back through Benghazi once more (for the last time) and on past the Gulf of Sirte, occupying Tripoli; and after the Anglo-American landings in North West Africa (November 1942) the last remnants of German and Italian forces were about to be driven from Africa.

A posting to a training establishment at this point in the war meant missing the forthcoming landings in Sicily and Italy, and wherever else the re-entry into Europe was to be. The middle East was now a backwater. It was frustrating to be stuck within a few dusty miles of where I had landed two years before. Furthermore, I was about to see many of my desert compainions pass through with formations who visited the Centre briefly in order to be put through their paces in landing operations.

I had made protests to Barkas and Medley and all the people who could have posted me back to an operational unit, but was assured that I was more use at the CTC. The snag about this was that the appointment of Instructor at the G2 (Major) grade, which I still held, was for a minimum of six months, and there was nothing I could do but make the best of it.

The daily routine turned out to be monotonous rather than over-taxing. Dennis Wootton had not shone as a lecturer; he was too diffident and nervous, although very able in other practical ways. I had, therefore, to reorganise the various standard lectures which were given to the staffs of the visiting units. The possibilities of concealment and decoys were shown by demonstrations and lectures, using a canvas model of a typical landing beach.

I had to get an epidiascope and other lecture props, but if the lecture hut (a tin nissen hut) was blacked out efficiently for use of the epidiascope it had became quite unbearable in the scorching

103

heat. The temptation was strong to rush through the lecture and get out into the open air, jump into the lake and cool off.

The office was a hut shared with two other officers – the Medical Officer, Jowett, and the Chemical Warfare Officer, Pip Bairstow. 'Doc' Jowett had acquired a small off-white mongrel dog called Pooch, very devoted to Doc and suspicious of me. Pip Bairstow was a very friendly and lively man with a literary talent. He composed a witty jingle about the three of us which started:

> Chemico, Medico, Cam, pom pom,
> Are really a terrible sham, pom pom,

which we sang to the strain of *He's gone and married Yum Yum* from *The Mikado*. We had acquired a sailing boat and spent much of our spare time sailing it on the lakes, landing on the various sandbanks to sun ourselves and swim. There was a steady stream of ships passing through the Canal, the channel marked at Kabrit Point by a line of huge bollards. I used to swim alongside these, gradually extending my distance. I made a sand-filled medicine ball with which I exercised regularly, and I began to feel very fit and brown as the summer developed.

There were, at Kabrit, a number of Naval characters who were training for some hazardous trip to the Dodacanese or other Axis-held island. They were to approach the coast in a submarine by night and then take to rubber dinghies from which they would, after daybreak, observe and sketch details of the beaches from which landing plans could be made. It seemed that all their bravery and skill in navigating their dinghies was likely to be let down by their inability to bring back intelligible records. I therefore devised a simple system by which they could observe the landscape through a cut-out framework, divided by a simple grid of wires and held in the free hand. This helped them to record accurately the subtle and fugitive details of horizon and coastline which a particular approach from the sea would pick up.

Drake Hard was one of the practice take-off points of embarkation for men and vehicles and represented the departure of the attacking force from the parent ship, to take place some miles offshore. The crossing from Drake Hard to the eastern shore of the Sinai Desert was the final run in and touch down. The training was to familiarise all arms – Infantry, AFVs (armoured fighting vehicles), Signals and Engineers – with the procedure for embarking, disembarking and assembling in their planned positions once ashore, and to iron out any confusion which might occur.

Combined Training Centre

Convoy carrying troops for the invasion of Sicily passing Kabrit (CTC) and Indian troops training disembarkation

Impression of night assault landing across Suez Canal. CTC Kabrit

Brig Chater, the Commanding Officer of the CTC, was a Royal Marine and reminded me very much of the mustard-keen RM Brigadier in Calais. Later I had reason to be very grateful for his unstuffy attitude when, on a trip from Syria, I was in trouble with the Military Police for leaving 'secret' documents (my lecture notes) in my truck overnight in a military car park in Palestine. He took the welcome line that the Military Police should have warned me that the military car park, although guarded, was not secure.

I soon acquired a cat which slept in my tent. In the Mess (a series of interlinked marquees) we were favoured by having Jack Byfield, an officer in the RASC, who used to play most beautifully on the Mess piano. Although I never met him again, whenever I heard him on the Radio in later years I was reminded of this hot stifling camp·

I tried to use my spare time (generally in the full heat of the day) to do some drawings and watercolours. The view through the perimeter wire outside my tent was of the arid hills of Sinai across the lake. At sunset these took on a fantastic but shortlived beauty, the low angled pink light picking out the form of the ragged hills and escarpments which at midday were flat and dull.

Sinai was a constant invitation to explore. I knew that far across to the east lay Petra, 'the rose red city half as old as time', with its Nabatean Hellenistic buildings sculpted out of solid rock. It was possible to drive over to visit Petra, but I turned this down in favour of a trip to Cairo when my leave came round. I regret the decision to this day.

The Suez Canal Company still occupied the main block of buildings on the promontory. Kabrit is the Arabic word for 'match', and I have always assumed that it was so named because of its shape on a map. It is like a matchstick stuck in the western bank. The garden on the point was unexpectedly beautiful, well irrigated and expertly tended, with some rare and heavily scented plants that I have failed to identify, particularly some lovely white blooms with a wonderful haunting perfume.

Later on I had the chance to penetrate a little deeper into Sinai than the few hundred yards covered during the landing practices. This was when I undertook to do a survey of a more extensive area and to produce a map for use in exercises. I was not really trained to do this but the procedure could afford to be quite rough and ready, taking a compass bearing on a distant high point, motoring over to it, recording the distance on the mileometer, and from there selecting another salient feature. As usual with the desert landscape, it was seemingly featureless at first but on more

APP.... DRAFT. Given with ectratics + editions
to No 2 PLANNING STAFF.

CI LECTURE TO PLANNING STAFF.   25 June 43. CTC.

My object in this lecture is to examine with you and clarify the possible
scope of camouflage in Combined Ops. That is to say, camouflage in the widest
meaning of the word " as any and every means of hiding or disguising yourself from
your enemy; misleading himas to your position, strength and intention, confusing
him so that he wastes his blows, and falls into your ambush ".

We may gauge the character and extent of the affects which it will be both
useful and possible to bring about, by ready reference to past experience —
both bad and good. We may then spot the main essentials which will here and now,
go to the making of original and effective cover plans for the forthcoming operations
with which you will be concerned.

Very probably, the most ambitious cover plan of this war - and quite possibly
of any war, was, as you well know, employed to introduce the element of surprise
into the battle of Alamein.

The implications of the scheme were most complex, and involved, on the visual
camouflage side of it at least, the fullest use of all existing means, and the
conception of new ideas and methods.

The basic object and effect of the scheme was no different in principle
from many other historical examples - Allenby's false build up of strength prior
to his successful reak through in Palestine in the last war, having obvious
similarities.

The methods were, however, indeed new in themselves, (and made use of many
technical principles which even eighteen months previously had never been dreamed
of, or dreamed of only by a few "specialists or experts" who were not infrequently
regarded as so "specialist or expert" (in the less polite sense of the word.) as
to be treated with open suspicion and ignored when they spoke on such "military"
matters as cover plans.

Let us therefore briefly examine the conditions which existed in the autumn
of 1942, among which there certainly existed the ESSENTIALS necessary for the
success of a cover plan of " campaign swaying" dimensions.
First. There was the SET PIECE. That is, a set of known Static Conditions.
Second. The INITIATIVE was in our hands. i.e. we were timing and placing
the attack.
Third. The Commander's real operational plan, not only allowed of, but
called for, a cover plan to give it a real chance of success. (Surprise, was in a
true sense an essential to success if the very strong enemy defensive disposition
was to be overcome.)
Fourth. This being so, what was the existing machinery and deceptional
data at the disposal of the Commander in forming his cover plan ?
Happily this was considerable, being the result of a years continuous
endeavour on tactical operational deception; tried and tested in current
operations.
Briefly, the following detailed experiments had already gone to make the
various instruments - as it were - of the full deceptional orchestra that was
ready to play at Alamein.

TOBRUK SNIEL.
Battle area. Enemy's attention focussed on Western perimeter by large
suspicious screen scheme, which he shelled heavily over the desired period when
the break out of the Eastern perimeter was to have been made.

D SERT RAILHEAD.
Large scale semi strategic Deception. Confusing enemy to date of
opening of CRUSADER Op, and distracting 50% of his bombing effort from the real
RH 6 miles away.
A later R.Head relied also on being a focal point of water supply,
including 30 miles dummy pipe line leading from the places of real importance.
Effect largely unknown, but pipe was attacked.

BLISH PROJECT.
This, In Feb 42 was the first really well backed and co-ordinated effort to
draw bombing from Tobruk and Benghasi. We planned to make a dummy port, where
Italians had already made and demolished port installations. We simulated repair
and development and much false activity including dummy shipping. This was
abandoned in the Feb withdrawal without compromise, and in a very promising stage.
Many valuable technical lessons learned.

......2.

Forward Bases.   A new outlook on the need for concealing the identity and state of completion of forward bases was established at Belhamed (itself a failure) May 42.   New and bolder methods to this end were thought out and became accepted la[t]

Army and Other Large Formation HQs.

In May and June 42 came the fuller realisation of the need for special precautions, groupings and dispersals, as a means of disguising their identity and preventing enemy, air borne attacks aimed at paralysing the control centres at critical stages of operations.   These developments are not being mentioned in any spirit of self satisfaction on the part of Cam, but to show the gradual awakening to the real meaning of the subject and the widening of its scope.

Most important of all was the change in attitude towards the desert as "background" in which to exploit camouflage.   From being regarded as a blank hopeless space where all home training becomes meaningless, and where good dispersal is the beginning and the end of the matter , it came to be accepted as an ideal place for the building up of "false pictures" and the cunning substitution of real for false, and vice versa in a kind of giant " Spot the Lady", in which the enemy air force became the unwitting stooge.

Meanwhile, much progress had been made in the design and quantity of production of standard decoy equipment of all types, and the Cam Branch at GHQ had grown sufficiently robust and experienced to play its necessary part.   METP No. 8 Pt IV, Operational Cam.   Notes on Planning for Commanders and Staffs, written and arranged from the foregoing experiences and published in October before Alamein, now read almost as a prophecy of Camouflage part of that battle.

Its appreciation of what are called the "Indispensible Partners in Camouflage " are as true in regard to forthcoming Combined Ops as to the then imminence Battle of Egypt.   The Pamphlet is still alive it its basic lessons still apply.   I confidently commend it to you.   That deals therefore with the Technical "ripeness" of the task.

FOURTH ~~Fifth.~~   The ~~fifth~~ next factor is TIME, which depends mainly on our holding the **initiative.**

When a false build up has to be undertaken, it is obvious that the C means to a satisfactory and gradual production of the desired (false) picture can only be successfully worked if sufficient time is allowed for the planning and the layout on of the necessary men and material and transport.

If the assistance of the Cam officer is required in the idea itself more time still is needed.

FIFTH. ~~Sixth.~~ Another ~~and last~~ factor is DIRECTION. i.e direction of the experimental or training effort by the planners, so that it is carried out economically and progressively to their desired end.   [handwritten annotation] denc print tot Oct 23

Let us now examine how each of these essential requirements for a good cover plan is ~~answered~~ presented in Combined Ops. Problem.

The "SET PIECE" is reasonably assumed. Moreover the INITIATIVE is ours, i.e. the timing and placing of the operation.

The nature of the real task suggests the particular need for a good original cover plan.

Time, (although possibly not as long as might be wished (it never is) should be sufficient, provided the right people are put in the picture early enough, the scope and limitations of available deception equipment fully understood by the planners.

Possible difficulties may be met with as follows :-

Whereas at Alamein the gradual accumulation of desert experiences - the gradu breaking of new ground - had all been done and could be readily applied - the partic nature of the Combined Ops problem forbids "trial and error" methods to a very large extent.

There are no current Combined Ops on which to learn.   It must be a "first timer".   All the more need therefore for exercises.   These may be very specialised secret, and carried out separately by special units, or they may involve the partici of the invasion formations in their own General Trg, and exercises.

In any case, to be sure of our schemes not miscarrying - through development, experiment, testing and exercising are necessary.

This calls for a healthy co-ordination, under the planners, of all these activi One cannot develop useful ideas without some guidance as to the limitations and conditions of the actual exercise involved, likewise one cannot train economically, realistically and usefully unless some guidance is given

.....3.

This is surely a question of so designing the rigid limits of security that they do not completely paralyze the working out of ideas. Ideas in past experience have not been lacking if given an encouraging breeding ground of essential and definite facts and conditions. Ideas in Cam in fact tended to outpace the ability of the army to use them.

It will not be any exaggeration to say that the success of an assault depends on who first gains the covering position in force.

From our side we may well be ~~pleasur~~ forced into becoming slow ~~or only part~~ ~~masters~~ by various mishaps and delays.

Here, surely then, is the supreme need for any and every measure which may confuse, delay, distract the enemy reserves who will be anxiously waiting to grab the covering position on any one of several coastal sectors in their area.

We have heard of the use of dummy parachutists, dropped away from an objective in Madagascar, who successfully drew off the only mobile enemy reserve whilst a landing was made elsewhere. The Hun probably also heard, and we must think of other ways and means. Some already exist or are under development, but they must be well ~~known to~~, and guided by the planning Staff, if these "gadgets" are to fit their task, and they must be incorporated early in a cover plan.

Too often, still, is an admittedly good scheme shelved because it is too late, and the allotment of available labour, transport or craft has been made, and re-allotment would cause too much of an upheaval.

The skilful and timely inclusion of deception teams and their equipment may well prevent something very much more unpleasant than a mild upheaval at a later stage. ~~Here and how one cannot discuss actual ways and means to this end. It would be the appearance of "speculation".~~ The possibilities are probably known to many of you and it is up to you.

I have not mentioned the scope of Cam for the Brick. This is considerable, but can and really must be laid on within the Brick itself. As at all levels, careful planning in the 1st Key Plan is the first essential, to make all possible use of the ground for concealment. Next comes good "directed" for the dump and other personnel in the time available, and, after the landing, comes the keen speedy recce of the actual site by the Cam officer (with the DAQMG) for the 2nd Key Plan, and finally the constant supervision and chasing up to see that the plan is actually followed.

This may be followed by improvised decoy dumps and fires to meet the situation. For all this to be done a Cam Officer is certainly required and is well worth a place in the party.   8.RTR decision

The morals and lessons ~~known~~ I have tried to bring out, briefly stated are :-
(a)   Realise the great need and opportunity for deception in combined ops.
(b)   Decide your cover plan early on.
(c)   Give your Cam Officer sufficient information, to enable him to make his appreciation and plan, and if accepted, to state his requirements in men, materials etc in good time.
(d)   Back him up fully in carrying it out.
(e)   Wherever possible give him a chance to have a few "ideas" of his own; he has been chosen for his job because of that quality he has, and has probably had to think up "fast ones" before.
(f)   "Guide" the development and training people sufficiently to enable them really to deliver the goods.
(g)   Remember it is probably a question of "breaking new ground". Subject to vital security measures, have full scale tests and exercises of all deception equipment and schemes, so that they will go smoothly on the day.

intimate examination revealed endless individual details and characteristics.

I soon came upon some quite extensive and well-preserved entrenchments complete with dugouts, just as I had always visualised First World War trenches to be, and that was indeed exactly what they were, constructed it seems, against the Turks. Deeper into the desert a dark sharply defined shape came into distant view, hard to identify as its scale was indeterminable and with a quite weird outline. I approached it with a strange excitement, and was disappointed to discover only a curious stunted tree, still alive in this dry dead place. There was a small depression around its trunk, and a tentative area of fallen leaves was forming a humus in which other small plants were struggling for existence. I sat in this hollow for a long time listening to the slight rustle of the desert winds stirring the tree, and slowly I noticed more and more little signs of vegetable and insect life. I wondered what chance had first allowed the seed to settle in this arid home, and grow.

I had experienced a similar excitement in the Western Desert when, after months of seeing no trees or shrubs other than the low camel thorn, I had perceived, far away on the Trigh Capuzzo, an isolated shape which proved to be a lovely fig tree. I had also once, near our camp at Depot 3, investigated a dark hummock on the horizon which proved to be a kind of gorse bush on a small sandhill which had collected around it from the constantly shifting sands; but what really astonished me was that growing round it was a broken ring of fungus. For all I could see, they were normal field mushrooms such as I had long delighted to find in English and Welsh fields.

Returning to the day-to-day routine at Kabrit, I went sick on 6 May and next day Doc Jowett sent me to 19 General Hospital where I stayed, with a very high temperature, until I was discharged one week later.

My successor at Eighth Army, Tony Ayrton, had died of meningitis towards the end of the long advance, and my old Staff Lieutenant, Brian Robb, had stepped up into the job. He now visited CTC with John Baker. After this I saw more of my old Eighth Army friends who were preparing to cross to Sicily, and the feeling of being left on the shelf became very strong. Diary comment, 'Baker's visit rather disturbing. Once more my job obviously pointless.'

I visited GHQ Cairo on 31 May and made another unsuccessful attempt to get away from Kabrit. Maj Buckley of the camouflage course at Larkhill was visiting from England, and I had dinner with him at the Auberge du Turf. He was in a much more amenable mood than at Larkhill. Next, George Vale of Eighth Army and Haifa passed through and, once more, Brian Robb and Johnny Codner. I gave them all help and information.

On 10 June my diary records, 'Simon two years old. Write lecture for Planning Staff. Very difficult – need for great tact.' The need for tact referred to the way in which suggestions for subtlety in concealment or decoy planning could be proposed to the Army or Navy planners without appearing to be teaching them their own business. Moreover, the claims of camouflage on the available resources of men, equipment and stores, as against the undeniable demands of the basic operation itself, were still difficult to assert.

11 June – Diary note, 'Get parcel off to Jean – textiles and sandals. Concert at Saunders. Talk to singer afterwards in Mess.' The materials and sandals were bought in the Muski (the native market) in Cairo. Saunders, where the ENSA concert was held, was a Naval shore station connected with the Combined Training Centre. There was intense heat and masses of flies. A pretty girl performer sang *Cherry Ripe*, perhaps a song not best suited to charm the average serviceman, but to make matters worse she had a huge fly constantly aiming, it appeared, to make its way into her open mouth as she sang. This brought roars of mirth from the audience which obviously embarrassed her, but she kept bravely on to the bitter end. I found her very appealing and was delighted to be able to talk to her afterwards. It did not take much to spark off a romantic sympathy in these conditions but, of course, the ENSA party went valiantly on their way.

Towards mid June I went to an establishment in Syria called No 3 Dryshod Wing. The activities were similar to the training at the Centre at Kabrit, the difference being that there was no water. I gave a talk and demonstration here, then on to 8 Royal Tank Regiment at Aartouz, north of Baalbek. The vehicle broke down and to my amazement we (my driver and I) were passed by Robert Medley conducting Col Buckley. A strange chance meeting – and just another of those desert coincidences.

I returned via Tel Aviv and while there I walked to Jaffa. Having my sketch book with me, I was sitting drawing in a café when an Arab beckoned me to follow him. He said I should draw his sister – a variant, at least, of the usual pimp's approach. He led me into a very ancient stone building, then into a small cell – one of many leading off a huge cavernous arched corridor. Presently a very beautiful Arab girl came in and, amid much giggling, was told that I wanted to make a picture of her. Of course money changed hands. My request that she should sit still was too much for her, and she began to pull at my sketch book to see the progress being made. She continued to pose more and more provocatively and was beginning to undress when a thunderous banging started on the huge entrance door; then a young Arab boy burst into the room and whispered dramatically 'Police, Police!' I was shepherded out by a back door – feeling very stupid.

By 13 July one year had passed since I left the Eighth Army. Around this time I was invited by some officers of the Jaipur Guards to a dinner celebrating an Indian Festival of the New Moon. I turned up at their camp (in the open desert, near Kabrit) just as it was getting dark and with a huge appetite – which I had been cultivating by fasting all day in readiness for the enormous curry meal I had been led to expect.

The Indian Officers, who did not themselves drink alcohol, regaled their guests with an array of NAAFI issue spirits which they had been saving for this occasion, and an endless stream of Mess waiters kept our glasses full of neat whisky and gin. There was an atmosphere of rather forced hilarity, and a very fat and jolly Jaipur Captain asked me repeatedly, 'What's yours' – then would clap hands and shout for whisky, gin or sherry, or all three. I admired his sandals – Indian Army pattern – and at once he clapped his hands and called to a Mess servant, whereupon I was presented with a pair of sandals. Those sandals were marvellous. I used them all through the rest of my Middle East service and for a long time after the war. No other sandals have ever been to satisfactory.

The drinking seemed to be over-prolonged, and then it dawned on me that the meal would not be served until every bottle was empty. When at long last we were ushered out of the tent to sit at a table set under the night sky, I was feeling drunk and unsteady. I was, however, still very hungry, and when the first delicious rice dish was offered, along with pickles and chutneys and other delicacies, I served myself lavishly. I hoped that sufficient rice would sop up some of the superfluous alcohol and save me from passing out. It seemed to help, but the next ordeal was having to eat what seemed an endless succession of richer and richer dishes – and more and more rice. To decline an offer of food seemed quite unacceptable to our hosts. In the sky the crescent moon was now plain for all to see, but in this Festival of the New Moon no deference to it was made and no ceremony followed. I staggered away eventually, still drunk and grossly overfed, clutching my sandals and wondering why this feast could not have been spread out over a month for our canteen meals.

My diary for 23 July records a typical description of the recurring training exercise across the lake: 'Land about 0515. Watch beach work. Up to see Pip's smoke screen at 0600. Visit beach again. Brick HQ etc signals. Make report back to office. Walk to decoy area and back. Very tired. Meet Col Robertson 2030. Sleep on beach.'

A Brick was a complete landing formation made up of all necessary services and units – Navy, Army, RAF. In the later Normandy landings it was known as a Beach Group. I remember on one such exercise forgetting to fill my water bottle. The idea that I had to go all through the day without a drink was appalling and yet I felt too proud to ask anyone to share theirs. I am sure imagination brought on the thirst, for within a short time I was parched and craving a drink of water. Normally I drank very little in the heat of the day.

By mid August a note of desperation developed in my diary. There were endless lectures, demonstrations and conferences – and a growing determination to get myself away from the CTC. I began writing in numbers, '15 August, 952', etc, these cryptic diary entries recording the number of days overseas. (They culminated in 1,000 on 2 October.) On the 954th day I wrote a DO (Demi-Official) letter to Col Barkas, again pleading for a new posting. Finally the monotony of my diary entries became too much, and there is a gap of two months.

At some time during this period I was given a belated chance to get away from CTC and return to the UK to join a unit preparing for the invasion of the Atlantic Wall. The condition was that I lose the rank of Major, which I had held since my appointment to Eighth Army in October 1941. So anxious was I to get away from Kabrit that I had, on a visit to a training establishment near Jenin, in Palestine, volunteered for training as a glider pilot. This hope was thwarted by some technicality connected with being of field rank.

At last, realising that all chance of getting back to an operational appointment in the Middle East had disappeared (all such units having gone to Italy) this was the only course open to me. I did not want to lose rank – for one thing the drop in pay from Major to Captain was very considerable – but to be left in a backwater after 1,210 days away seemed totally unacceptable.

Before I left Baghdad some of the 'artist camoufluers' planned an exhibition of paintings. Sandy Barclay Russell was one of the prime movers in this project, and very successful he was. Soon afterwards his talents for organising cultural activities and exhibitions were given full scope when he joined the British Council. He was a character who seems to have stepped straight out of Olivia Manning's *Fortunes of War*, his very long shorts and long moustache giving him an early explorer look, and he was always festooned by his equipment – webbing, pistol in holster, binoculars, compass and one of those huge multi-purpose penknives beloved of scout masters.

The exhibition finally ran just after I left Paiforce, so I never saw it. To my surprise and delight I received news that all my work had been sold. Barclay Russell later organised a much more ambitious United Nations Art Exhibition in Cairo, which was opened by King George of the Hellenes. I again sold several works.

I finally left Kabrit on 16 January 1944, and went to Cairo, where I had a pretty typical last few days in the Cairo playground – Groppis, Turf Club, Opera, etc. I also had my chessmen plated in the Cairo Muski. I had, over many months, made a chess set out of a variety of rounds of ammunition which I had collected, Allied and enemy, and they were very simply sculpted at the open end of the cylinder by cutting, curling and twisting the metal cylinder wall. It was necessary to do something to differentiate the sets and I decided that, rather than paint them black and white, I would have them plated – gold and silver. All the ammunition had been emptied of its cordite so there was nothing (I thought) left to explode. I had replaced the bullet tops in the case of the pawns, but had not fired off the caps in the bases, and the Arab plater managed to make a cap explode, causing full scale panic in the surrounding stalls.

When I went to collect the work on 18 January I was told vivid stories of how this had caused great amusement in the Muski! It was the sort of thing that appealed to the Arab sense of humour. I bought a very suitable ebony and ivory box which, when opened, provided the chess board. I had been playing a little chess towards the end of my time at CTC and bought a book to study the classic openings. My new set was to be much used on the ship home.

The next day, 19 January, I left Cairo for Alexandria (having been joined by Doc Jowett at Cairo Station) and boarded *SS Ranchi*, which sailed on the 20th. The voyage, according to my diary notes, seems to have been mainly dominated by chess, with occasional variations such as '31 January, stay up and watch passing neutral or hospital ship – lit up'. On 7 February, 'Land visible at first light. 0845 N Ireland. Evening anchor Gourock.'

114

We had to hang about on board for nearly three days watching US troops getting priority in disembarkation and, indeed, being officially welcomed (which we were not!); but on 10 February, our fourth wedding anniversary, I at last disembarked from the *Ranchi*. The voyage out on the *Samaria*, Liverpool to Tewfik took 85 days; the return, Alexandria to Gourock, 21 days.

My memories of that *Ranchi* voyage are of Felix Harboard singing *Alice Blue Gown* and organising games of 'tick' or 'it' round the deck, eyed most disapprovingly by senior officers; and the magic of the passing lit-up ship. We had not seen anything lit up for so long. I had organised a 'chess ladder' on the voyage and became so engrossed that the arrival at Gourock, in spite of the excitement of being back in the UK, was almost a frustration. I was unbeaten and had climbed seven places! I have never played with such intensity since.

As soon as I was able, after leaving the ship, I telephoned Jean in Formby. We had missed celebrating our fourth wedding anniversary by only a few hours, but I was back on UK soil after 1,241 days overseas.

9

Before going home to Formby I went straight to London to join Jean. I discussed a hotel with Felix Harboard, and he said he would ring the Ritz where he had reserved a suite of rooms throughout his period in the Middle East. He offered to arrange for us to have a room there, and that is where we spent our reunion. The room was vast – it probably seemed more so after tents and overcrowded ship cabins, and I thought we could well have lived quite comfortably in the closet wardrobe which had a long line of empty coat hangers. Jean, who had been ill for our last stay in London – our honeymoon just over four year ago – was suffering from a bad attack of pink eye (conjunctivitis) which upset her and spoiled some of the happiness of the reunion. After one or two nights at the Ritz I found a smaller hotel where we felt more at home.

Then back to Formby. My father, who was 69 on 29 April 1944, seemed as fit and active as ever. I remember wrestling with him in fun, and his arms had a vice-like grip from which I could not escape. My mother, on the other hand, had suffered a slight stroke; she was much changed and spent a lot of time in bed.

Jean had been living about a mile from our family home in a semi-detached house facing the open fields and the distant pines. My Great Aunt Edith had died during the war and my mother had bought her house, so Jean, Simon and Jean's mother, Mrs Judd, had moved there. My father was a constant visitor, and a great closeness had grown up between him and 'the little man', Simon.

My first experiences of fatherhood were not very encouraging. I took Simon for a walk to the shore and tried to get him to enjoy what I, myself, remembered enjoying as a child – tracking in the pines and jumping down sandhills. Instead he starting crying and complaining and I lost patience. Poor Simon, it turned out that he was suffering from an abcess in the ear. He was only two years and eight months old, and the sudden appearance of a strange man in the house must have shattered his familiar routine.

Jean had a part time job teaching pottery at the Liverpool School of Art and I visited her there, watching her turning some of her pots. I had done just this, or watched her throwing or glazing, when we were both at the Royal College of Art from 1933-36. This side of her life had obviously helped her in the face of a very monotonous and stifling amount of domesticity – surrounded by her mother and my parents, all doting on 'the little man'.

We do not seem to have done anything very notable during my 14 days' leave. A walk to the shore on the final day sounds like a re-take of the January 1941 departure, and indeed proved to be the prelude to another lengthy separation.

Back on duty I paid a visit to the Camouflage Development and Training Centre at Farnham Castle, and was shown the impressive development of the mass manufacture of dummy and decoy equipment. Then, on 8 March, I reported to 21 Army Group, which turned out to be a rather deflating experience. The office to which I had to report was in Brook Green, near St Paul's School, where Monty and his HQ had attracted some recent air raids. A young officer, who I took – from a quick glance at his shoulder tabs – to be a full Lieutenant (2 stars), told me to follow him. We went down a passage, into an office – whereupon he sat down at the desk facing me and started to tell me just how wrong I was to think I knew anything about camouflage, or even the Army – how the whole deception business was now to be run 'professionally'. He was, I realised, a Lieutenant Colonel (a star and crown, not two stars!) He said he understood I was familiar with combined operations (amphibious landing) and this being so I was to report at once to No 5 Beach Group near Elgin.

I still do not know what made this young man so hostile to the returning Middle East camouflage veterans. Perhaps he suspected resistance from Geoffrey Barkas' Circus. Barkas had been recalled to the War Office some time before.

Oddly enough, having escaped any very serious insect bites during three years in MEF, I now had a very painful leg due to a bite in a railway sleeper between Liverpool and Euston. It became septic, swollen and very painful. Therefore, after leaving 21 Army Group I searched for an Army Medical Post to get treatment, but the dressing which the orderly put on my leg, just above the knee, slipped off almost at once and I found myself disentangling the bandage around my ankle.

That evening I caught the train to Scotland, where my welcome at No 5 Beach Group at Loch-Na-Bo, near Elgin, was cool. I was by now wearing an Africa Star Ribbon, the undistinguished version without the metal numeral 8 on it which was reserved for post Montgomery members. Perhaps this counted against me, as a rift had grown up between returning Middle East forces (or other theatres of war where there had been action, such as Burma) and the home based troops, who had been waiting up to three years without seeing any action. The 5th Battalion of the King's Liverpool Regiment was indeed in this category.

Beach Groups (the UK equivalent of the Middle East Bricks) were carefully balanced units of all arms, with Naval and RAF elements, formed around an existing infantry battalion. They were designed to land the assault troops and from then on to defend and work the beaches, to keep the advancing troops supplied with ammunition and all else that they needed. Coming from Formby, at least I was a local, and it was comforting to hear the scouse accent again. Once the ice was broken we found that we had friends in common, and I discovered that I had played pre-war for the same Liverpool Schoolboys Rugby XV versus Manchester with John Langdon, one of the Company Commanders.

The previous Battalion CO had recently been removed from command, and since he was popular with the Battalion and a local man also, his successor, Lt Col Board from another Infantry Regiment, was somewhat resented. But his time with the King's was not to be long. He was killed, along with his batman, before getting off the beach very early on D Day.

On 10 March I contacted Capt James, Adjutant of HQ Company, and discussed training requirements. I also met Basil Spence (later the architect of Coventry Cathedral) who was the Camouflage Officer (Captain) on 101 Sub-Area, the formation in control of 5 and 6 Beach Groups. We had lunch together and he told me that he was hating his job at Sub-Area – he had no freedom to do camouflage and felt only a stooge. I had met Basil and Joan Spence, and their two children, before the war while I was working for two years for Herbert Hendrie in his stained glass studio in Edinburgh.

My leg was now giving serious trouble and eventually I went to the Pinefield Infantry Training Centre Casualty Receiving Station, where I was given a bed. I nearly passed out with leg pain in the evening and tried to re-dress it as it was bleeding. The hole in the leg was now about the size of an old penny and deep. I stayed at the Casualty Station for several days, and had here a VAD nurse who was the nicest I met in all my hospital visits during the war. She invited me out of my small room to sit in the Nurses Mess, where there was a radio and easy chairs. I enjoyed my time at the CRS – and especially the lovely hot baths. The only disadvantage was that this was an Infantry Training Centre and bagpipe practice took place outside my window.

On 21 March I returned to Beach Group HQ and to a 'Leap Year' exercise briefing and conference. Leap Year was the code

118

name for the D Day landings rehearsal, which took place from 26 March to 1 April. My little unit for the landings was to consist of myself, a Sergeant, a draughtsman Corporal and a jeep Driver. Sgt Parkin was the first to arrive. He was a very large Guardsman, a very reassuring fact in view of the fast approaching landing.

For security reasons there is a total lack of detail about the D Day rehearsal in my diary, and in keeping a diary at all I was to some extent breaking security restrictions unless it could be completely uninformative on military matters and unspecific to a boring degree. I developed a compromise technique which I could amplify later from the clues offered, and this I have now tried to do.

After a number of complicated conferences we were broken down into small parties according to the landing craft we were to join. The training document concerned is entitled *Allocation of units to ship and landing craft (by units) and Landing Table Index*. I have it still in my war album.

I have no record of the other units which were to sail on this tank landing craft (LCT) (type 4). The main cargo was, of course, the tanks. The LCT 4 held nine, and there was a large metal locker at the stern end of the tank compartment which would provide cover for the tank crews during the voyage. It was known as the 'army shelter' and had no comfort whatsoever. Due to the need to cram as many troops as possible on the available landing craft, all kinds of small parties were also put on the LCTs. For them there was no cover unless they could infiltrate into the crew's quarters.

In theory a quick trip across the Channel in June sounds very agreeable; in the event, on 5-6 June, it was cold, rough and most unpleasant. At midday on 28 March we went aboard our LCT from the hards at Chanonry (near Inverness) but alas, there were no tanks embarking for this exercise and the LCTs were more than ever unmanageable. We put to sea, but next day, 29 March, it was rough, very cold, and the rehearsal was postponed (indeed, this proved to be an accurate rehearsal for D Day itself). The postponement was not much of a relief, for it meant we would be aboard so much longer. As this was not planned, we had no means of combating the extreme cold. I do not think I slept at all in the army shelter, in which there had already been a lot of seasickness.

In the morning we got away, and although it was still choppy we completed our sea mileage (the equivalent I suppose of Newhaven to Normandy) and at 1615 hours we approached the coast. There had been some kind of real bombardment earlier and this had set fire to some pine woods and marram grass on the sandhills. By the time we landed there were squads of Land Army girls beating out the fires, which tended to spoil the realism. The craft should have run right up on to the beach which would, when the ramp went down, have allowed us to run through a foot or so of water, on to the beach and away to our first objective.

To our dismay the craft hovered just short of the beach, went astern and began to twist sideways. The ramp went down amid yelling from the bridge above, and the troops pitched themselves off the end of the ramp into some five feet of freezing cold sea. Just ahead of me I saw QMS Edwards of the King's HQ Company, who was a very short man, disappear completely for a few seconds before he emerged and struggled up the sand. Once on the beach I thought my lungs were going to burst from the extreme cold. I started running to try to get my circulation going, but the compressed feeling got worse. Then I realised that I had forgotten to deflate my Mae West life jacket, which was under my webbing equipment, and its pressure was preventing me from drawing breath.

Once ashore we had to establish a Beach Group HQ and begin to organise the landing and dumping of stores, etc. After dark the Sergeant and I scooped a hollow in the side of a sandhill, covered it with a sheet of corrugated tin, and piled sand over the edges. We had settled down in this, were trying our most unappetising emergency ration pack and had begun to conjure up a little cosiness, when we heard voices approaching. An officer rapped our tin roof with his cane and snapped, 'Get that cover down. No shelters allowed.'

The exercise seemed interminable, and not particularly helpful or realistic since so much had to be make believe. No doubt, however, many administrative wrinkles were ironed out as a result of 'Leap Year'. The veto on cover could not have affected the Beach Group HQ, which was in a tent; when I sneaked in, pretending some urgent business, I found they had acquired a stove. I stood as near to this as I could and must have fallen asleep for a spell, standing and leaning on the tent pole. I awoke befogged as to where I could be, hugging the tent pole for support. The only other time I have slept standing up was in the cabin of the *Ben Lawers* on the voyage back from Calais. I also remember very clearly the bliss of the hot bath I had back at Loch-Na-Bo.

About a week after this ordeal (compared to which the purely physical side of D Day was a pleasure) the Beach Group – the 5th King's from Loch-Na-Bo and the family of units from their surrounding camps – all moved south to their assembly camps for

120

the invasion. The journey south was via Aberdeen and Newçastle, arriving at Emsworth in the afternoon of 11 April. We had iron rations, but had depended on station stops for cups of tea. It is extraordinary what a vital part tea played in our lives. As we shunted round London on some secondary line all the housewives seemed to be brandishing tea pots out of their windows, saluting us with mysterious yet meaningful gestures. Considering the gigantic flow of troops to the south at this period they must have been doing this for weeks. At our earlier stop at Aberdeen we had lined the platform with our mugs and queued (officers last) for the tea urn. A few places ahead of me it dried up, and although the urn was whirled away to be replenished, the train pulled out before it reappeared.

The other tea stop was in London. It was only years later that I suddenly recognised that it was Addison Road Station in West Kensington, where we again queued with our mugs. This time the urn was commanded (not serviced) by a Guards Officer with a shiny metal-edged peak to his cap. Surely this time all would be well. But no – again the supply failed.

We left the train at a small country station (which turned out to be Emsworth) some 25½ hours after leaving Elgin, and were taken in trucks to a tented camp nearby. The whole countryside was occupied with camps, tents sited carefully under trees, and endless tanks, SP (self-propelled) guns and military vehicles of all descriptions lining the roads and lanes. I noticed that they were correctly parked under trees – the only snag was that, in April, the trees were completely bare.

The final assembly camps in the south had been given a big build up with the troops while we were still in the north. The food was to be superb. There were to be all kinds of comforts and non-stop cinema shows – but later we would be 'sealed' in our camp and the security would be complete. Anyway, I expect I finally got my cup of tea. The food was about the same as any other army food. The non-stop cinema turned out to be a true fact, the only snag being that it was a non-stop showing of the same film. It was not a bad film – a Hollywood musical, with masses of stars, called *Thousands Cheer*. You could hear it grinding away endlessly from all over the camp. I used to rouse myself and look in at the cinema marquee when it came to Lena Horne's song *Honeysuckle Rose*.

The security was tight, but I remember one or two outings. I gave some lectures – probably about regulation concealment training for dumps. We did some route marching from Camp A2 near Emsworth, carrying the equipment we expected to take with

121

us on D Day. There was some elasticity about what personal things could be put in one's kit, but the military equipment was, of course, strictly specified. One essential was a heavy entrenching tool, which made good sense in the circumstances. I still had only a pistol for personal protection or aggression. During a halt in one of the route marches I sneaked off and hid a quantity of personal property where I could come back and collect it later, so intolerable had my load become. I had developed a rheumatic shoulder, which made things worse, so I began to parcel up just about all the private belongings I had and posted them home to Formby. A curious sense of freedom developed once there was virtually nothing left. I did, however, keep my rather cumbersome Voigtlander 120 bellows camera.

Camp A2 was the main camp into which the whole of the 5th Battalion King's Regiment and the 5 Beach Group HQ had moved, and we stayed there from 11 April until just before D Day when, on 2 June, we split up to go to our various final pre-embarkation camps. The one I went to was coded J2 and was situated somewhere near Lewes, west of the Lewes-Brighton road. It was an estate, complete with ancient hall and outbuildings where we had our Mess. We slept in tents under avenues of trees, which now were in full leaf. I took a photograph of some kittens which peered at me from a loft there. The final camp was sited near to the Embarkation Port, in our case Newhaven, and was a very temporary shakedown. The family owning the estate had recently died out, but they were remembered in the little graveyard in the grounds.

On 3 May I had a puzzling and rather undermining experience. My small party and I received detailed rehearsal orders to proceed to a Box in Portsmouth. The term Box, unlike the all-round defended Boxes in the desert, referred to a temporary holding place for embarking troops. It was so near A2 at Emsworth that only a short transit period had to be catered for. We collected blankets and had a meal, then on 2 May and again on 3 May we marched to the hards to embark. What worried me was that we embarked on an entirely different kind of landing craft from the LCT in Scotland – an LCI (Landing Craft – Infantry).

This would indeed have been much pleasanter during the night crossing as LCIs were purpose-designed to put infantry ashore in the best state for the assault. Each man had a bunk and there were good messing facilities, etc. Knowing that something had gone wrong I reported to the PBM (Principal Beach Master), who held the key to the very complex loads and embarkation details. As I feared, it had all been a mistake – so we had no final rehearsal of the embarkation.

I went to the Beach Sub-Area HQ for final detailed briefing where, displayed in a marquee, we saw photographs of the area of the D Day landings, but the actual identity of the places was still kept secret. However, I very soon recognised the area as being the coast near Ouistreham and the area inland from there to Caen. The Abbaye aux Hommes, St Stephen's Cathedral, and the Abbaye aux Dames were familiar, as was the canal itself for I had visited and sketched there with my brother, David, a few summers before. We had taken the ferry boat then from Le Havre, and the little paddle steamer entered the canal in Ouistreham, sailing the few miles south to Caen through the very Normandy fields which were to become so familiar after the airborne landings.

I felt excited and rather smart to have recognised the place and even thought my knowledge might have some value. So I reported it to the senior briefing officer. His reaction was alarming.

'Have you told anyone else?' he asked.

'Certainly not' was my reply.

'Can you undertake absolutely to keep your knowledge entirely to yourself till the landings are under way?'

'Yes', I replied.

Only then did he relax and tell me that if I had divulged the information I would have gone straight to prison along with anyone I might have told.

Another memory of this place was that we had meals in a marquee and that the tea included spring onions.

On 17 May I went to Chichester with Peel, an officer of the King's Regiment. We travelled by car from the Portsmouth direction, which gave us a most impressive view of the cathedral across the open land to the south. I remember browsing through bookshops and eventually choosing something for Simon's third birthday on 10 June – with a feeling of apprehension for I was fairly certain that, before he received it, the invasion would have taken place.

We also visited Bosham and saw some of the large concrete caissons (to be used in the Mulberry Harbour) sitting in the creek – plain for all to see. The success of the security for Overlord (the invasion operation) still amazes me.

22 May was notable for an inspection by King George VI, and for this we formed up along with hundreds of other units, and waited. I can remember hearing, rather than seeing, the King and the inspection party approaching. When they were a few yards

short they stopped and I could hear the King's rather fruity voice commenting on a 'fouled anchor'. I could make little sense of this and the temptation to look to the right to see what was happening was very considerable. Then the party continued on its way and in a second had passed. It was long enough, however, to get a strong impression of a very tanned monarch.

After the parade I discovered the reason for the hold-up in the inspection and the conversation I had heard. Beach Groups wore a special Unit sign on each shoulder, below the distinguishing title of Regiment Corps and the appropriate colour flash. The sign consisted of a pale blue disc with a red band encircling its edge, and in the centre was an anchor. This fouled anchor had a length of rope draped round it in a double bend, forming an S or a reversed S. We were issued with one of each, with strict instructions to wear them always with the fouling rope curving forwards at the top. I found it very remarkable that the King should have spotted the unfortunate member in the front rank who was wearing identical signs – therefore incorrect. Even if His Majesty had been tipped off to look for such a shortcoming, it still demanded very sharp sight to see so small a detail.

On 23 May I met Col Belchem and Oliver Poole, (Conservative Party Chairman post-war) who had been at Eighth Army HQ in the desert and were now in 21 Army Group HQ. They were friendly and expressed sympathetic surprise at my reduction in rank.

I also contacted my brother John, now a Captain in the Royal Marines and commanding 538 LCA (Landing Craft – Assault) flotilla. His small assault craft were to make the crossing on a parent ship – a sizeable cargo vessel called the *Empire Broadsword* anchored at Portsmouth. I went aboard and was given dinner by the Captain (Capt Patchett) and John, and I was able to make out that we were, in fact, to land within the same hundred yards of beach. His craft were to be lowered into the sea some seven miles out and boarded by the assault infantry by clambering down nets hanging from the hull, then to make their run in to the beach in close formation. John's LCAs were identified by a clear BD (Broadsword) on the hull. Capt Patchett kindly presented me with a bottle of whisky, and this I concealed from the dockyard sentries (liable to search shore-going servicemen) by contriving a broken arm in a sling – an excellent camouflage officer's hide for a bottle.

By now all those involved with the D Day landings, or the follow-up were getting utterly sick of the waiting period, so when 2 June brought a move to J2 Camp it was welcomed as a sure sign that something was about to happen. It also meant parting from our familiar companions of the Beach Group, who we would not see again until we were on the French beaches.

The stay at J2 should have been very brief, for on 4 June we boarded trucks and were driven to Newhaven. Before the war I had crossed to France several times from Newhaven but had never seen it looking as it did on 4 June 1944 – the whole harbour was solid with landing craft. One could have walked across the harbour in almost any direction from ship to ship.

It was comforting to be back on the familiar LCT 982. The ship's officers were the Captain, Lt Cooper, Midshipman Ware, Engineer Officer Darbell, and the Flotilla Officer, Lt Cdr Humphreys. The Army Shelter was no more welcoming than it had been in north Scotland and now, of course, the full load of tanks and their crews made things very crowded. I remember the babble of voices and radios, British and American. It was a relief when the craft filed out to sea.

Such a concentration made one feel very vulnerable. I pictured similar choked harbours all along the south coast to east and west. Surely at least one German reconnaissance plane would get a glimpse of it and the whole operation become known. The daylight lingered till after 2200 hours at this time in June.

The landing craft assembled some miles off the coast and dropped anchors. This, we supposed, was part of the plan, forming up into the correct order for the voyage to Normandy. The LCTs were tossing and twisting in the choppy sea and the problem of where to go soon arose as it had on the rehearsal in March. The Army Shelter was full of the tank crews and small parties from other units, and in order to get some rest many men had stretched out on the open deck or in the cover of the tanks.

Presently the ships hauled up anchors and got moving once more – but to our dismay we realised that we were heading back to Newhaven. Many versions have since been told of the dilemma faced by those responsible for setting the whole huge and intricate operation into irreversible motion. They must have known the inevitable reaction of the troops already aboard the armada and the anticlimax a postponement might cause – also the extra difficulty of maintaining surprise, as some units had already gone ahead, such as the midget submarines which were to lie offshore and mark the beach approaches prior to the assault.

We spent the night aboard, back in Newhaven, and on the morning of 5 June the news spread that there was a 24-hour delay. We were ferried back to J2 Camp in lorries. According to my diary

I sunbathed, visited the kittens in their loft and then, in the evening we returned to the LCT, again putting out to sea. It was still rough and windy, but this time the whole huge group of vessels formed up and headed steadily south.

The 6 kittens at Camp J2

10

I have frequently marvelled at the complexity of the D Day operation. Thousands of different units with their respective and unique functions had been shepherded from all over Britain and delivered to their correct ship at the correct time. The ships had foregathered from ports all round the British Isles and now were proceeding in the correct formation, and at the correct speed, to deliver their various loads of men, guns and tanks, together with all the complex impedimenta of invasion, at the right sector of beach at the right state of the tide – to be followed day after day by the follow up of supplies and reinforcements.

There was a full moon at 0658 on 6 June, I do not think it ever got really dark – certainly the nearer part of the armada of ships could be seen ploughing along in formation. Up till this moment the maps and operation orders of Overlord had not been disclosed. The packets containing them could now be opened, so that the bogus maps used in training – with their code names familiar to all – could now be identified with the true place names.

I have preserved a number of the documents for D Day and most of the photographs and maps, notably the Bogus Map showing the BMA (Beach Maintenance Area) layout, with our sector named Cairo. This had all the features, roads, houses, woods, etc marked on 1:25000 scale, and the numbered layout plan was overprinted in red. The First Key Plan was the key to all the 77 sites or areas. I have also kept a fragment of the actual Overload operation orders cover, with a waggish Lord, complete with coronet appearing over the cartouche containing the title Overlord – giving the Victory sign with his left hand, and a rather ominous downward pointing with his right.

The Intelligence Officer of 5 Beach Group was Ernest Quinn of the King's Liverpool Regiment. He had managed to make the earlier Intelligence conferences very lively, frequently turning very Nazi when describing movements of German troops, assuming a convincing Teutonic delivery and much clicking of heels. It certainly made news of the arrival of two Panzer Divisions in the Caen area seem a little less depressing, and his publication of the various operation orders, including 'Leap Year, had some delightful graphic touches.

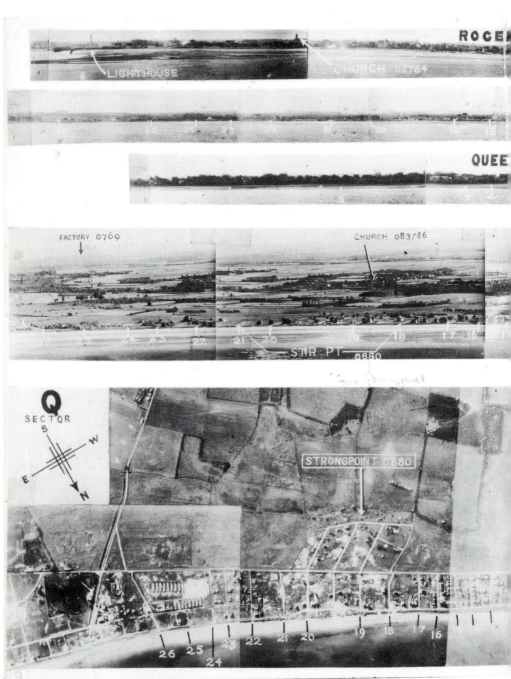

Briefing documents. Sword sector. Roger and Queen a) oblique (wave top) photos, b) low obliques, c) vertical

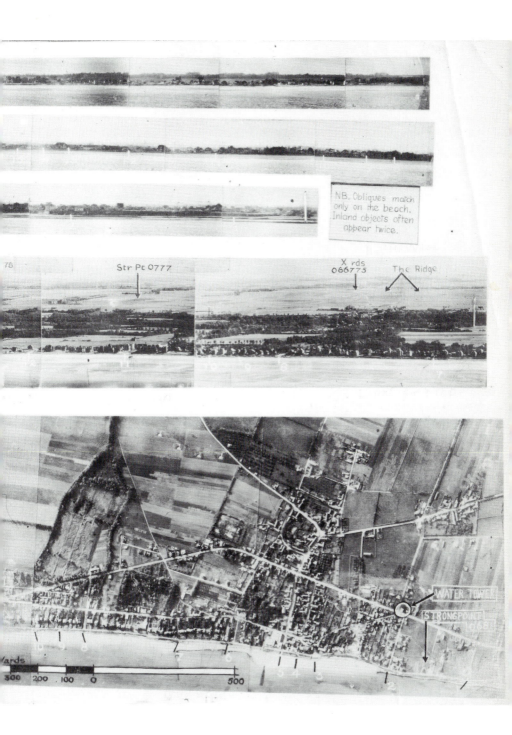

NB. Obliques match only on the beach. Inland objects often appear twice.

78

Str Pt 0777

X rds
066775

The Ridge

WATER TOWER

STRONGPOINT

Yards

300 200 100 0   500

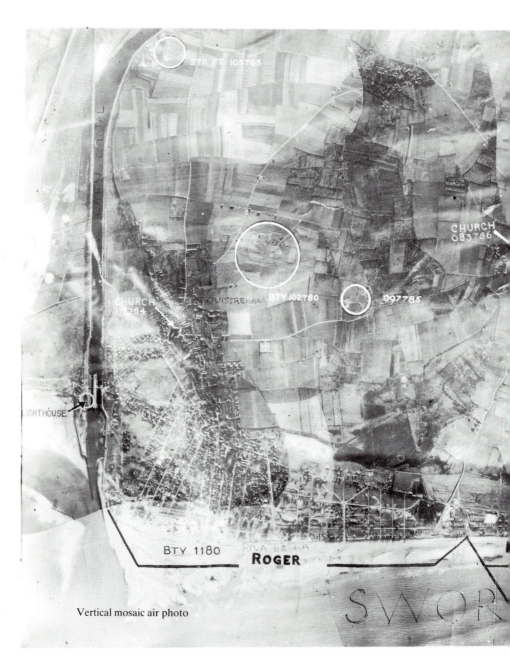

Vertical mosaic air photo

130

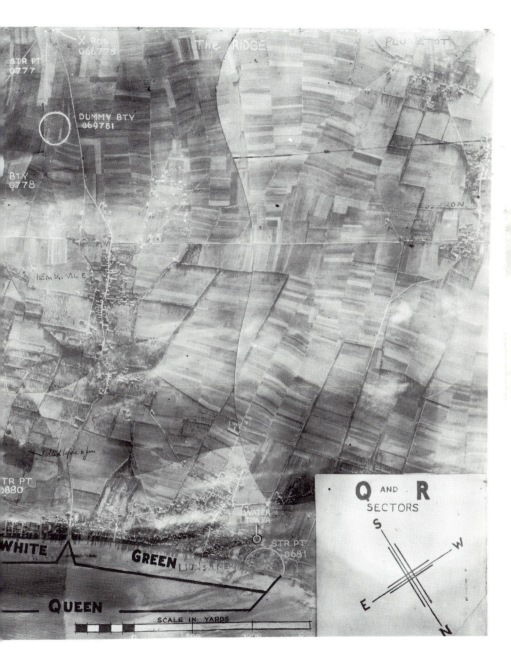

The air photographs were on two sheets. One had horizontal wave-top views of the whole series of beach sectors, pieced together in sequence and over-marked in white, with the sector number and such landmarks as the Ouistreham lighthouse and church with map co-ordinates. There was on the same sheet a strip of low-angled horizontal air photographs, on which the characteristics of individual villas on the front could be distinguished, and the details of the hinterland could be broadly discerned. Photo reconnaissance aicraft had flown at wave-top height a considerable time previously to photograph these beaches.

The third strip was a true vertical moasic taken in good clear sunlight with indicative shadows and the position of the 0880 Strongpoint (destined, we hoped, to become 5 Beach Group HQ) clearly ringed. The name of the Beach was Queen Sector. The point I had to make for was between 18 and 20, just inside Queen Red (the 0880 Strongpoint).

Roger Sector extended eastwards from Queen Red to the Caen Canal entrance at Ouistreham and was the most easterly point of the seaborne landings. The British Zone of Assault had three main parts, east to west. They were: SWORD. 3rd British Division; JUNO. 3rd Canadian Divison; GOLD. 50th British Division.

There was already a lot of seasickness aboard LCT 982 and I decided to clear my mind on what to make for on landing before I too became affected. I could distinguish two tall French seaside villas very close together on the photograph, the only place, in fact, where this spacing occurred, and I decided to look for these as the LCT drew close to the beach. There had been much demolition of the seaside villas by the Germans in their defensive preparation and this had continued since the photographs were taken – but the two tall, closely spaced villas were still there. Realising that the beaching of the LCT might be some way off target, I also memorised other points which I hoped to be able to check on.

There were still some long hours of waiting, and I hoped to stick it out on deck where I would be less likely to succumb to seasickness. At some point in the voyage a very fast and manoeuvrable landing craft came alongside and a very senior officer delivered a rather jingoish address through a loud hailer before passing on to repeat his message to other craft. Soon I got so cold that I decided to take cover and found a place in the engine room, where it was very warm but with a suffocating smell of hot oil. The crew seemed to have no objection, so eventually I lay down across the top of an engine cover and got some sleep. The vibration of the whole structure was such, however, that I gradually began to slip off as soon as I relaxed, and in the end I decided to go back on deck.

At first I could see very little of the rest of the invasion fleet. The sea was rough and the sky cloudy and dark, but before long I began to pick out the shapes of other craft moving along in formation. Aircraft were passing overhead in considerable numbers, but I could not tell if they were the airborne forces or bombers. Remembering the landing experience in Scotland I asked one of the tank officers if I could go ashore on a tank – thinking that I would at least be dry and that the tank turret would give some protection at the landing stage.

The officer was quite agreeable, but pointed out that parts of the tank were waterproofed, so that should it have to enter deep water it could not become waterlogged. Where the turret met the top of the tank hull was sealed too, but a length of Cordtex fuse was laid under the waterproof seal which, when set off, would blow the waterproofing compound clear as it burned. The turret obviously had to be able to come into action directly the tank was on the beach, so there was some possibility of being injured by the exploding Cordtex.

I wondered how my brother's ship, the *Empire Broadsword* was faring. The LCAs, of course, would be landing first, along with the amphibious DD (Duplex Drive) tanks, which also 'swam' ashore from some distance out at sea. DD tanks could be propelled by a screw in water as well as by the caterpillar tracks on land. Our landing time was H + 195 – that is, 195 minutes, or three hours and 15 minutes after the initial assault started (and incidentally at about the time of full tide).

In anticipation of the beach landings there had been lively arguments within the Beach Group about what, in fact, would prove to be the least, or most, hazardous time to arrive. Some had worked out that, in view of the huge sea and air bombardment sustained right up till the first assault wave reached the shore, they would have it easy, and that the men coming in later would be met by a recovering German defence. We would soon find out. The sound of the Naval and aerial bombardment, a deep sustained boom, could soon be heard above the noise of the LCT itself.

The Normandy coast was slowly changing from a dim line on the horizon into recognisable features, the undulations of the country behind the beaches visible at first, then blocks of woodland, and finally the villas, the Ouistreham lighthouse and church tower all began to appear as they looked on the wave-top photographs.

Ht. Lion

Chau

Clos Cobé
Gasholder

Lion-sur-Mer

HEDGE CLEARING

B^s Lion

ELEMENT 'C'

PROBABLE MINES &
WIRE ALONG SEA FRONT

HEDGEHOGS

NARROW STRIP OF EVEN SAND DUNE

15' MACADAM RD. LEAVES BACK OF DUNES
30° GRADING THROUGH DUNES REQUIRED.

NARROW RDS. BETWEEN HOUSES LEAD FROM BACK
OF DUNES. 30°-35° GRADING THRO. DUNES REQUIRED

15' MACADAM RDS. FROM BACK O

FLAME THROWERS

PATHS TO POOR RDS. AT
30°&40° GRADING THRO

8   9 10 11

13 14 15 16

17   18

NARROW METALLED
DUNES 28-30 YDS
200 YDS. WIDEN

PINE WOOD
felled before b|un
used to treate hidden
o 0880 ₧

Hermanville
sur-Mer

M.T BAYS

X

X

X

X

X

Colleville - sur Orne

EXCAVATIONS

HQ

X

WK

WK

WK

TOWER

X

ABANDONED

X

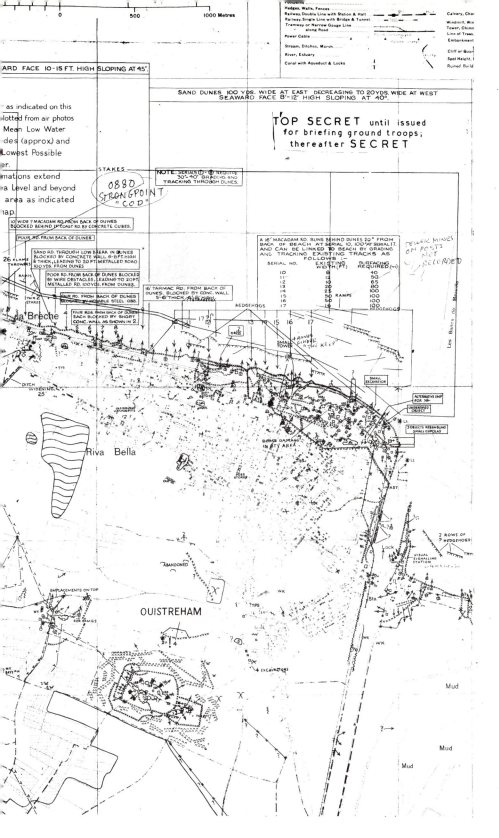

Without having come to a decision about taking the lift on a tank, I was now distracted by my efforts to find the two tall villas and to see where the LCT was going to touch down in relation to them. I also noticed an almost solid jam of armoured vehicles lining the strip of narrow beach, the tide being nearly full. The engines of the tanks were by now all roaring; then the ramp crashed and splashed down, and ashore they went. I followed close behind them on foot, the water being much less deep than in Leap Year.

My own small party consisted of Sgt Heath and Sapper Birch. Poor Birch, a very young and recently married man, had been seasick most of the way over and could only just make the effort needed. I had reckoned, in the last few minutes of the run-in, that we would have to move quite a long way to our left to get to the 0880 Strongpoint, and we started to run from the cover of one stationary vehicle to another, feeling very exposed to the menacing tall villas facing down on us. There was only a narrow fringe of low sandhills between the beach and these houses, and we could assume that they were fortified. As we leap-frogged along we kept seeing familiar faces of Beach Group troops, and when we dropped down beside other figures lying in the cover of tanks or trucks I suddenly realised that many of them were not, in fact, taking cover at all, but were motionless.

George Appleton, Commanding C Company of the King's, who had landed ahead of me, told me later that he had sprinted off the open beach and dropped down under the lee of a sandbank beside another soldier. 'Well, that wasn't too bad after all,' he commented, without looking at him. He got no reply, and looking sideways he saw that the man's head had been blown almost off his shoulders.

After some hundreds of yards we reached a point just short of the two tall villas where, beside a large blockhouse, the exit track from the beach was being frantically worked on. This was at the north western side of Strongpoint 0880. The exit track was being surfaced with wire mesh to stop the vehicles' wheels from sinking into the soft sand. Men were still at work on this although some vehicles, and certainly some tanks, must have made their way off the beach some time before.

The large German blockhouse was sited to face westwards across the open beach which we had just crossed. It had already been captured and converted into a CRS (Casualty Receiving Station), and the turf covering its concrete top had been pushed off and heaped up to block the firing aperture and rear entrance. There was a dead German lying on his back in front of the seaward

D. Day

H + 195 min. Queen 0880 Strongpoint. Barrage balloon still up

A little later. Queen White/Red. 5 Beach Group working on exit

D. Day

All round gun 0880 Strongpoint. 2 tall villas beyond

Scorpion tank stopped by Blockhaus anti tank

Rear of Blockhaus converted to C.R.S. Turf from top used to close gun aperture

Blockhaus anti tank front view. Dead German gunner in front

Dummy house over Blockhaus. 0880 Strongpoint

Major Winterton, Steven Sykes, Capt James 0880 Strongpoint

List 'A'

1. Det 21 Army Gp MC Pool
2. 84 Fd Coy RE
3. 8 Stores Sec RE
4. 999 Port Op Coy RE
5. 50 Mech Eqpt Sec RE
6. 101 G T Coy RASC
7. 96 DID RASC *Detail Issue Depot*
8. 237 Pet Dep RASC
9. 20 FDS RAMC (incl Surgical Team)
10. 21 FDS RAMC (incl Det 1 Fd San Sec)
11. 39 FSU RAMC *Field Surgical Unit*
12. 40 FSU RAMC
13. 21 FTU RAMC *Transfusion*
14. 1 CEP RAMC (½ 30 FDS) *Casualty Embarkation Point*
15. 11 OBD RAOC *Ordnance Base Depot*
16. 44 Ord Amn Coy RAOC
17. 20 Beach Rec Sec REME
18. 53 Coy Pnr Corps
19. 292 Coy Pnr Corps
20. 303 Coy Pnr Corps
21. 102 Coy Pnr Corps
22. 241 HQ Pro Coy CMP
23. 'F' Commando RN
24. 17 Beach Sig Sec RN
25. 101 Beach Sec RAF
26. 50 Balloon Unit RAF
27. Spare
28. Spare
29. File
30. File

List 'B'

31. HQ Coy 5
32. Sp Coy
33. A Coy
34. B Coy
35. C Coy
36. D Coy
37. File

List showing composition of Beach Group

140

BEACH Gp.

'C'	List 'D'
2 i/c	58. CO
Adjt	59. 2 i/c
QM	60. Adjt
IO	61. Lt Col EA Carse
SO	62. Staff Capt
MTO	63. Staff Capt (Camouflage)
MO	64. S & T
PMC	65. Docks Supt.
Mortar Pl	66. IC
Carrier Pl	67. QM
A/Tk Pl	68. BOWO
Pioneer Pl	69. File
RSM	
Chaplain (C of E)	
Chaplain (C of S)	
Chaplain (RC)	

War Diary

File

'E'	List 'F'
HQ 101 Beach Sub Area	80. 6 Beach Gp
HQ 8 Inf Bde	81. A Coy 1 Bucks
HQ 185 Inf Bde	82. B Coy 1 Bucks
HQ 9 Inf Bde	83. A/Tk Pl 1 Bucks
6 Beach Go	84. 1028 Port Op Coy RE
'M' Assault Gp RA	85. 299 G T Coy RASC
DNOIC 101 Beach Sub Area	86. 9 FDS RAMC
3 Reece Rugt (Traffic Major)	87. 12 FDS RAMC
2 Middlesex (Traffic Major)	88. 3 Br Inf Div REME
File	89. 21 Beach Rec Sec REME
	90. 601 Coy CMP (VP)
	91. 'R' Commando RN
	92. 102 Beach Sec RAF
	93. File

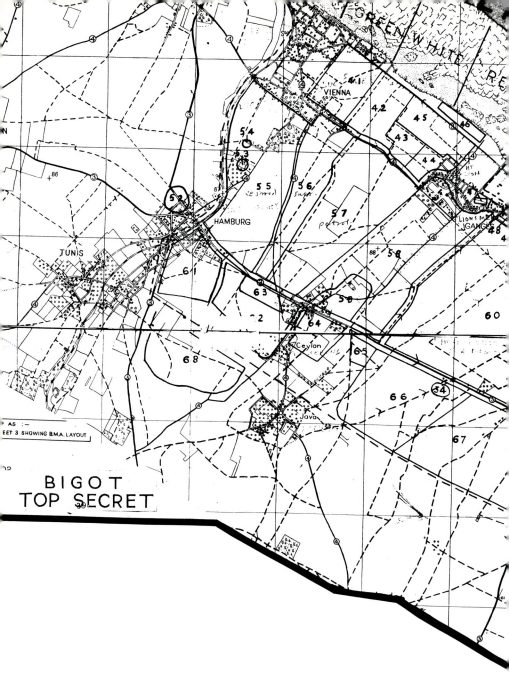

The numbers refer to positions of the areas etc on First Key Plan (following page)

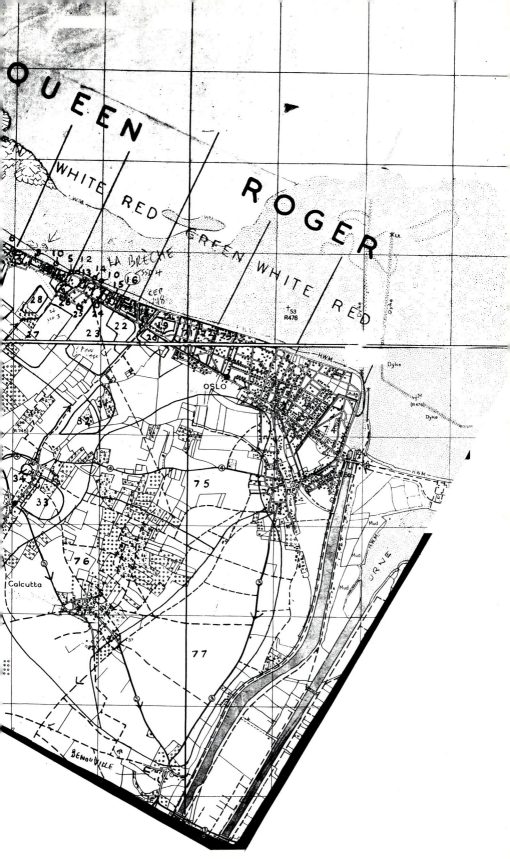

First Key Plan

LEGEND

1. Transit Areas D Day Personnel.
2. "   "   "   " Wheeled: RN
   Veh pk D+1.
3. Transit Areas D Day Tracks.
4. Bivouac 1.
5. DUKW Control Point
6. BDS and BRC
7. Sector Stores Dump 1.
8. "   "   " 2:CRU on D+1
9. DVP
10. Beach Coy HQ
11. Bivouac 2: CRU in NE Corner D Day.
12. 5 Beach Gp Comd Post.
13. "   "   " Main HQ.
14. 101 Beach Sub Area Comd Post.
15. DVP and REME HQ,
16. Sector Stores Dump 4: CRU on D+1.
17. Bivouac 3.
18. CEP   Casualty Evacuation Point
19. Tn Dump.
20. Burial Area.
21. Wheels Control Point.
22. RE Bridging Dump.
23. PW Cage.
24. Stragglers Post.
25. Water Point.   W Air Tower
26. Sector Stores Dump 3.
27. 20 and 21 FDS,   Field Dressing Stations
28. Bivouac 4: RN Camp D+1.
29. HQ 101 Beach Sub Area.
30. Gen Tpt Park,
31. REHQ and Bivouac 5.
32. Pnr HQ and Bivouac 6.
33. Burial Areas.
34. Porpoise Dump.
35. HQ 73 LAA Regt.
36. Main DVP.
37 - 40. Spare Numbers.

41. RE Bivouac Area.
42. Pnr "   "
43. S & D Coys 1 Bucks Biv Ar
44. 629 A Fd Coy & RE Sec Biv
45. Spare Bivouac Areas.
46. Burial Area.
47. PW Control Post.
48. HQ RASC and Report Centre
49. HQRA,
50. HQ 6 Beach Group.
51. RAP 1 Bucks.
52. AMOR.
53. HQ 103 HAA Regt.
54. Water Point.
55. RE Stores.
56. Sups.
57. Pet.
58. Ord.
59. G.1098.
60. Amn.
61. CCS.   Casualty Clearing Stn.
62. 1st Rfts.
63. 1st Rfts Tks.
64. 9 and 12 FDS.   Field Dressing
65. Burial Area.
66. Extension Area.
67. Docks Gp Biv Area: AVRE
       rallying Area.
68. Civilian Refugee Camp.
69. Simplex RN.
70. Spare numbers.
71. Transit Areas D+1 Personne
72. "   "   " Wheeled.
73. "   "   " Tracked.
74. Army Tn Units Area.
75. Assembly Area FIELDING: I
       Eastern corner.
76. Assembly Area HOMER: DEFOE
       Eastern Corner.
77. Assembly Area CONRAD.

      Traffic Post
> > > > Circuit Arrow.
------------- Inter Beach Gp Bdy

Letter 'A' in front of number denotes site if Plan 'B' comes into force.

side, and at the back, just where we stopped to take stock of things, there was a pile of bodies, both German and British. I wondered what the single dead German had been doing there *in front* of the blockhouse. I had brought my camera with me, strapped to the chin strap of my steel helmet to keep it out of the sea, and at this point I quickly took one or two photographs of the scene.

Sapper Birch was still looking very green so I left him in a small well-protected German machine-gun post and went on into the Strongpoint. As I remember it, the 0880 Strongpoint was roughly the size of a football pitch. It lay along the top of the fringe of sandhills overlooking the beach to the north, and was bounded to the south by a road running parallel with the coast.

The blockhouse already mentioned was on the western and seaward corner of the beach exit along what could be regarded as the goal line. There were other large concrete pill boxes on the sea touchline – at the halfway line and eastern corner. There was a medium gun in an open pit, sited to fire all round the area, and also many underground dugouts, some quite large and containing stores. In the south-western corner, alongside the road, was an elaborate pill box disguised to look like a house, and all were connected by deep, narrow trenches.

About six of the original French villas had been left standing – and were expected to be heavily booby-trapped. I did not, of course, understand this layout so clearly at first, although I had seen the pattern on the defence overprint. The first dugout I went into contained a badly wounded German, and I followed with some apprehension the very deep, winding trench which had long grasses growing out of the side walls, obscuring the view ahead. I came to a long dugout – empty but containing a German sniper's rifle, which I took along with me.

When I had followed the communicating trenches to their ends, I returned and took Birch and Heath into the first dugout. The Beach Maintenance Layout Plan had shown the Beach Group HQ on two sites in the sandhill strip near the Command Post. This was understandable at the time the plans were drawn, as it could not then be assumed that we would find vacated enemy dugouts ideally situated for occupation. The Beach Group HQ people had made some attempts to dig in at the official spots indicated, but the Acting CO, Maj Winterton, with the Adjutant, Capt James and IO Ernest Quinn, then moved into the German dugout which I showed them, and they set up the HQ there.

I also conducted the Battalion RSM (Regimental Sergeant Major) round the trenches, and this time we came to a point where a knocked out tank had crashed through a dugout roof. It had collapsed a section of the adjoining trench, blocking the way, and the body of a German was half buried beneath. The first dugout (cleared of the wounded German) was now filled with King's HQ men, and it was at this point that I heard of the death of the CO, Col Board and his batman. It is strange to reflect that in the whole of this area, in and around the Strongpoint, there were relatively few bodies, dead or wounded.

I now set out to see how I could do useful work in my role of Camouflage Officer. The pill boxes had been overrun and silenced, and the all-round-defence gun in the centre of the position was shot through, with jagged holes in the protective shield. There were the few German corpses I have mentioned, and I had also come upon a dead English officer from the Lincolnshire Regiment, lying face down with his tin hat tipped forward cupping his face, revealing the back of a close-cropped head with a neat wound plumb in the centre. It seemed that the Lincolns of 3 British Division had assaulted and cleared the place along with the tanks, and had advanced inland. The King's had then moved in, some very early and some later, but they had not occupied the Strongpoint before I got there at H + 195. I wondered where the rest of the defenders were – prisoners most probably, but they were nowhere in sight.

I reported back to the Command Post, still on the open fringe of sand dunes. The beach was a fantastic sight, craft of every description being signalled in to the beach touchdown positions by Beach Control, Naval and Military. Large coloured wind sock markers had been erected to help the ships in. These later began to attrack enemy fire and had to be lowered, as had some barrage balloons along the beach edge. Strangely enough, I was not conscious of being shot at in spite of snipers still operating from the houses, and some shelling and mortaring.

One of my first practical tasks was to find some drinking water for the Medical Officer, who was looking after the casualties in the CRS bunker. I got this by wading out to a landing craft which had discharged its troops and was about to leave.

The jam of vehicles on the beach, denser along to the west where I had landed, was now moving steadily inland. The tide, which had) been about full when I landed, leaving a very narrow strip of sand, was now widening as the sea dropped. A Flail or Scorpion tank had been knocked out near the beach exit and this, with other damaged vehicles, had caused blockages in the earlier stages. I helped to recover a 6-pounder anti-tank gun which had gone down in deeper water but could now be reached and hauled out.

My diary entry for 6 June only reads: 'D Day. Still rough. Up 6 am. Land faint. Little fire. Recognise beaches. Land H + 195 to right of White. 10.30 (early) SA fire. Complete jam of vehicles. Commander killed. Also Lts Scarfe and Symes. Night on beaches. Save 6-pounder.'

I lost all sense of time as one task followed another – mostly obvious needs to be dealt with in the landing of stores and getting them forward to their correct dumps. There was a complication here – in the first few days the full dispersal plan for ammunition, petrol and other stores could not be carried out because there was a German strongpoint holding out between the 3rd British Div Area and the 3rd Canadian Div further west. This was at a place called Petit Enfer, a strange name for a village but appropriate as it turned out.

The dumping had to be done, therefore, in a much more concentrated area. The SSDs (Sector Stores Dumps) were designed for a rapid 'over the counter' service to the forward troops, so that very little would accumulate there. The area directly behind the beach houses and roads was waterlogged, with few access tracks. This limited the alternative dump areas and, in the event SSD sites – particularly SSD3 (directly behind the 0880 Strongpoint) which became dangerously congested and impossible to camouflage.

I do not remember returning to the crowded dugout that night. I must have eaten some rations but I did not sleep. This was no hardship, I was so stimulated by the realisation that the invasion had happened, was happening and progressing, and that I was still part of it. The beach was where our job lay. A few miles inland the assault troops were heavily engaged and for them to run short of ammunition, petrol or supplies would be disastrous. There had been talk in the evening of Caen being captured, then rumours of fierce fighting much nearer the beaches, and wild rumours about the strength of the continuing resistance at Petit Enfer.

In the evening there was a parchute supply drop to the 6th Airborne, just across the Canal and River Orne. The parachutes were in many colours indicating their load and they looked very lovely in the evening sun. The aircraft turned to the west after the drop and seemed to fly quite slowly and low, right over the very section of coast still held by the Germans at Luc and Lion-sur-Mer. I saw at least one hit and set on fire as it pulled away over the sea.

7 June D + 1. The King's had now moved into the original dugout and there was no room for us, so we moved on to a larger dugout which no one had annexed, near the eastern corner of the

Strongpoint. I then invited Peter Wiggins to join us. He was the other ex-North Africa campaigner who was the Chemical Warfare Officer (as I was the Camouflage Officer) and we felt a certain kinship.

The beach work and arrangements controlled by the Beach Group were going well. The dugout I had taken over was particularly well chosen, for it must have been a ration store and we found tins of pumpernickel, sauerkraut and other German rations, also a very nice miniature peg chess set. I spent most of the day on the nearest SSD, which lay just across the road behind the beaches – exactly opposite the Strongpoint. The area had a strange grid of small roads – rhomboid in plan – in contrast to the lateral waterfront tracks intersected by service roads at right angles. The holiday homes, for which this development had quite recently been made, had (except for one or two) been demolished by the Germans in order to preserve a clear field of fire at the rear of the Strongpoint. There was a water tower still standing, while behind was open country, with fields classed as 'boggy' on the map, with groups of trees dotted here and there.

Ernie Quinn joined me on the dump where I was struggling to make some sense out of the densely packed ammunition and petrol which was piling up. Ernie said there was truth in the rumours of German snipers lying low and still active, picking off odd people as they went about their work. From this evidence it seemed that the shots were coming from an isolated goup of trees in swampy fields, some 300 yards away. I still had my sniper rifle and we set off to try and flush out anyone who might be lying up there. My driver, Fitzsimmons, had arrived safely on D + 1 with the jeep loaded with the rest of our kit and equipment, and he settled into the new dugout. Quinn and I drove round the eastern side of this swamp area, skirting Ouistreham and keeping parallel with the Canal, and then took a rough track which led towards the suspect trees. We found nothing and the trip proved a complete anticlimax – for I think we were feeling the need for something more exciting than work on dumps.

I again spent the night working on the beach with Peter Wiggins, and he suggested that it would be nice to grab a bath on one of the huge landing ships which were now coming to the beach. These landing ships were more like small coasters and had bows with tall doors which opened to each side before the ramp came down. They carried a large number of vehicles. Wiggins seemed to know quite a lot abut these ships, and he assured me that they had good bathing facilities.

The ship we approached was far out, grounded at low tide, so we had a long walk across wet sand. As we reached it, towering above us, I shouted to a figure looking down from the rail, asking could we have a bath? We had no answer, for the roar of low-flying aircraft sent us surrying for cover – not on the ship, we assumed that was the target, but back across the open sand. Before we reached the cover of the sandhills and dugouts a stick of bombs straddled the beaches. We finished up in a crater caused by some previous action – and we forgot the enticement of our intended baths.

The air superiority of the Allied Air Force meant that the Luftwaffe only managed intermittent sneak raids. These, however, could prove very effective on a long densely concentrated, line of stationary shipping alongside beaches crammed with transport and dumps. At dusk the Army lit smoke cannisters along the coastal road, and as there was then an offshore breeze the targets were hidden in smoke. It occurred to me, however, that since the smoke source started along one edge of the target area, it would be a safe bet to drop the bombs just inside the line of the smoke. I was also puzzled as to why dusk was considered a particularly dangerous time. Needless to say, the troops in the beach area, and indeed the crews of the beached craft, would congregate in a long line just landward of the offensive smoke, presenting an even more concentrated target.

8 June, D +2. Diary recorded 'SSD3 hit. Three quarters burnt out. Help save MT and fight fire for three to four hours. To new ammunition and supply dump. After sniper in Hermansville. Wiggins wounded. Col Sale badly.'

The German plane which dropped a bomb right into the overcrowded SSD3 was being chased by a Spitfire. His one bomb was most effective. I was in the dugout when the bomb exploded, and I ran out to see what was happening; already a huge fire was starting in the dump about 50 yards away. In no time the fire had spread to the ammunition, which then began to explode rapidly, spreading the fire all over the area. There were some three ton lorries parked on the track leading into the dump, and as yet they had not caught fire. I tried desperately to start one up and reverse it away but made slow work of the job as I was unfamiliar with the starting procedure and gears. I did, however, shift two vehicles before it became impossible to approach.

All available Beach Group troops were called out to help contain the fire. The only way this could be done was to encircle the fiercely blazing and exploding centre and try to beat out the new

D + 2 Shelling on Queen White

Bomb burst on Queen White

SSD3 hits by bomb

Burned out petrol after bombing

fires which were igniting in the rest of the dump. There were some slit trenches among the piles of ammunition boxes. I crept into one, which was half filled with 3.7in AA ammunition, and crouched down ready to jump out and beat out with a shovel any new fires. Presently I heard an odd whirring sound above the general din, ending in a heavy thud in the next section of the trench, and I saw that a smoking shell case had landed beside me.

After more than three hours the fires had burned out or been stifled, but the exploding ammunition had taken it toll. Col Sale, commanding the neighbouring 6 Beach Group (Oxford and Bucks Light Infantry) had just taken over command of 5 Beach Group, and he was severely wounded. I had spoken to him for the one and only time as we went to the dump. Peter Wiggins had also been wounded, luckily not too seriously. He told me later that he felt a great fake, as he had been taken back to England and treated as a great D Day hero.

This bomb might have proved disastrous to the supply situation if it had been repeated along the coast. As it was, we were already opening up a new ammunition dump, sited close to the western fringe of the houses in the old Normandy village of Hermanville, marked 60 on the Beach Maintenance Area Layout. I went there after the episode of the burning dump, and all seemed spacious and peaceful compared with SSD3. From this dump several of the houses in the northern end of the village were visible, and a narrow lane led past the dump towards them. There was a huge and very deep crater nearby made by a heavy bomb, and on the very rim of the spoil there was a slit trench and a bivouack tent. This had been occupied by a soldier when the bomb landed, and by some extraordinary chance of fate he had survived. There was, it seems, a kind of 'safe zone' near the edge of a really deep crater.

I had not been working on the camouflage of the dump for long when there was a commotion in the lane. A Corporal had been shot, and again the sniper scare broke out. Before he was taken away I asked the wounded man to tell me all he could about the circumstances of the shot. From what he said it seemed probable that it had come from the upper back windows of a rather large old house, visible above an orchard screening one side of the lane. A search group was formed and a systematic examination was made of all the houses, occupied or not. The village people were full of advice as to the source of the trouble, and some of them insisted on us toasting 'La Liberation' with a glass or two of the local Calvados. I was soon to learn the potency of this, to me, unknown liqueur.

From their account there had been two sisters, 'blondes

152

Parisiennes – très jolies' – who had been collaboratrices, living with German officers partly in Hermanville and partly in the Beach Defences. One had been killed during the bombardment alongside (literally) a German officer. The other was still in Hermanville. I was directed to the house and as soon as I entered it from the street, I recognised it to be the one overlooking the dump area. An old, rather uncouth woman let us in and there, sure enough, was the attractive blonde. I was pleasantly drunk by now, thanks to the Calvados, and I felt sure the sniper was in the house. The most likely rooms were at the back, and I went up, full of anticipation, to a kind of lumber room or attic at the very top. It was full of old furniture but the search revealed nothing. Moreover, the small window was covered with cobwebs and clearly had not been opened for some time. In one of the bedrooms we found some binoculars and some spent rounds of 9 mm German ammunition. This, however, had not been fired recently.

I can remember carrying out a kind of interrogation which seemed, to my Calvados-warmed mind, to be very expert. The French word for binoculars, 'jumelles', came readily to my tongue, and the blonde produced a sullen explanation for both these and the ammunition. I reported the whole incident to the Sub-Area Intelligence Officer at the camp on the far side of the village; he said the blonde was already under observation and in view of events would be put in the POW cage.

On D +1 and D +2 considerable numbers of German prisoners were marched down to the beaches to be embarked on empty landing craft and sent to England. Of the photographs which I took at this time one shows the first Divisional Commander to be captured and his Staff escorted by a diminutive Tommy. The Commander's Aide remonstrated excitedly but ineffectively when he saw me photographing his boss. These prisoners had been sent in from all the surrounding areas where the Airborne Division and 3rd British Div had been in action. Some must have been from the beach defences. The first POW cage shown on the key plan as at 23 was certainly not actually formed there, for this was exactly alongside the ill-fated SSD3 and next to the 0880 Strongpoint. These crowds of prisoners appeared quite suddenly and the sight cheered us all; some wags started singing *Wir fahren gegen England*, the popular anti-British Nazi song. I believe that quite a large proportion of the troops manning the actual beach defences were Polish and other East German nationals such as Lithuanains, and they would in many cases have been very happy to be out of the war.

D. Day + prisoners assembled for shipping to UK

The sniper business had now started up all over again and there were so many groups forming up to retaliate that it was getting dangerous. I tried to get someone to co-ordinate the sniper-hunts, and went with one or two others to check out the building over in the centre of Hermanville which had been used by the Germans as a HQ. The rooms were all empty, still bedecked with Hitler's portrait, but there remained a cellar to investigate. This was entered by raising a trap door in the pavement of the footpath alongside the building. We had some German stick grenades which I had picked up in the HQ and, raising the trap, I dropped one in and stood back waiting. Instead of a normal explosion a deep boom like a depth charge sounded from below, and when we opened the trap a strong smell of cider wafted out. It seems that most orchard owners in Normandy have such vats for cider making, and I wondered what the stick grenade did to the flavour of the brew!

Meanwhile, the other party who were working through the garden at the back and the outbuildings had flushed out a real sniper – or at least a German. He was dressed in civilian clothes and had been wounded in the leg. In the garden shed, from which he had just run, we found a quantity of German uniforms. He was taken to the dressing station and I contacted Ernest Quinn, so that the circumstances of his capture would be known.

Back on the beach we were having a wonderful view of the battleships, lying not so very far out; they were shelling as called for by troops in contact with the Germans inland. These were good old-fashioned heavy battleships, ideal for this kind of support, and their heavy Naval guns could reach targets far inland. Some long ships which looked like LCTs were, in fact, mass rocket launchers, and they came quietly nosing inshore at the eastern flank, then suddenly let fly a whole phalanx of rockets on to the still active German coastal positions beyond the Orne. However, I believe the visual effect outdid the material damage, for I was to be involved with these very defences later, and they did not seem to have suffered much damage.

One memory of this time is meeting a lone Frenchman in the open country, and as if by magic he presented me with a bottle of wine and broke into enthusiastic but such fast French that I could not understand a word. Nevertheless, the wine was deeply appreciated. Such meetings carried a kind of symbolic and very moving significance, and the bottle of wine was a tangible bonus to be enjoyed in the dugout. Quite a number of French civilians were making their way into Hermanville now, and were shepherded to the area numbered 68 (Civilian Refugee Camp) provided for on

Message-urgent

du Commandement Suprême des Forces Expéditionnaires Alliées

AUX HABITANTS DE CETTE VILLE

Afin que l'ennemi commun soit vaincu, les Armées de l'Air Alliées vont attaquer tous les centres de transports ainsi que toutes les voies et moyens de communications vitaux pour l'ennemi.

Des ordres à cet effet ont été donnés.

Vous qui lisez ce tract, vous vous trouvez dans ou près d'un centre essentiel à l'ennemi pour le mouvement de ses troupes et de son matériel. L'objectif vital près duquel vous vous trouvez va être attaqué incessament.

Il faut sans délai vous éloigner, avec votre famille, pendant quelques jours, de la zone de danger où vous vous trouvez.

N'encombrez pas les routes. Dispersez-vous dans la campagne, autant que possible.

PARTEZ SUR LE CHAMP !
VOUS N'AVEZ PAS UNE MINUTE A PERDRE !

SAFE CONDUCT

The German soldier who carries this safe-conduct is using it as a sign of his genuine wish to give himself up. He is to be disarmed, to be well looked after, to receive food and medical attention as required, and is to be removed from the danger zone as soon as possible.

PASSIERSCHEIN

An die britischen und amerikanischen Vorposten: Der deutsche Soldat, der diesen Passierschein vorzeigt, benutzt ihn als Zeichen seines ehrlichen Willens, sich zu ergeben. Er ist zu entwaffnen. Er muss gut behandelt werden. Er hat Anspruch auf Verpflegung und, wenn nötig, ärztliche Behandlung. Er wird so bald wie möglich aus der Gefahrenzone entfernt.

Polacy w Armii Niemieckiej

PRZEMOC wcisnęła Was w szeregi śmiertelnych wrogów Polski, po katowsku znęcających się nad naszym Narodem. Przemoc narzuciła Wam mundur niemiecki.

Każą Wam bić się z oswobodzicielskiemi armjami wolnych narodów, szturmującymi zachodni wał t.zw. „fortecy Europy." Wraz z Amerykanami, Brytyjczykami, Kanadyjczykami, Francuzami walczą tam nasze Polskie Siły Zbrojne.

Wielu z Was otrzymało już wskazówki, czego od Was oczekuje Polska.

Rząd Rzeczypospolitej

- Gdy musicie strzelać — chybiać celu.
- Przy pierwszej okazji przechodzić do Wojsk Sprzymierzonych lub chować się, by doczekać się ich nadejścia.
- Rzetelnie informować Sprzymierzonych, gdy wejdziecie z nimi w styczność.
- Z chwilą znalezienia się po stronie Sprzymierzonych meldować żeście Polacy, prosić o oddzielenie od jeńców niemieckich i zetknięcie się z władzami wojskowymi polskimi.

Oczekują na Was bracia Wasi walczący obok naszych Sprzymierzeńców o wyzwolenie.

Niech Żyje Polska

Z.G.10

Calling
S.O.S
GERMANS
SEND US
DOCTORS

Allied and German leaflets collected from hedges and fields in Normandy

GENERALE PROKLAMIEREN RIEDENSREGIERUNG!

lin, 21. Juli : In einer Radioansprache
I Uhr morgens gab Hitler zu, dass
gestrige Proklamation der Friedens-
vegung von führenden deutschen
eralen stammt.

ering befahl der Luftwaffe, gegen die Bewegung einzu-
reiten und erklärte, dass es sich um „abgesetzte deutsche
erale" handelt. (Von Hitler bisher abgesetzt : Feld-
schalle v. Leeb, List, v. Rundstedt, v. Bock, v. Brauchitsch,
erale v. Falkenhausen und Halder). Von Seiten Goerings
Doenitz' wurde sofort nach Hitlers Rede der alten
hsregierung Gefolgschaft erklärt. Keine derartige
lärung erfolgte vom OKH.

iedensregierung gab Wehrmachts-Befehlshabern in- und
halb Deutschlands ihre Proklamation und Befehle
it. In Deutschland werden Flugblätter verbreitet, die
en, dass es unverantwortlich sei, den verlorenen
noch länger fortzusetzen und dass die Stunde
Handeln gekommen ist.

er wurde an Stelle von Generaloberst Fromm zum
Ishaber der Heimatarmeen" ernannt. „Generaloberst
an wurde zum Generalstab des Heeres berufen.

FEST STEHT FOLGENDES :

1. Dass die deutsche Generalität am besten weiss, wie die militärische Lage ist.

2. Dass die deutsche Generalität zu der Einsicht gelangt ist, dass Deutschland den Krieg verloren hat.

3. Dass die deutsche Generalität daher verlangt hat, dass man Frieden schliesst.

4. Dass die deutsche Generalität, als ihrem Verlangen nicht entsprochen wurde, selbst handeln musste.

5. Dass es in Deutschland jetzt eine Friedensregierung gibt, gegen die Goering „gewarnt" hat.

6. Dass zu dieser Friedensregierung die erfahrensten und bestinformierten deutschen Generale gehören.

WAS DAS FÜR DICH BEDEUTET :

Du weisst jetzt, was die Generalität seit Wochen gewusst hat—dass Deutschland den Krieg verloren hat. Die Friedensregierung mag niedergeschlagen werden oder nicht, an dieser Tatsache rüttelt niemand mehr.

Jede deutsche Reichsregierung muss kapitulieren, um Frieden zu schliessen. Die Bedingungen sind für dich und deine Kameraden durch althergebrachtes Kriegsrecht und die Genfer Konvention geregelt. Die Generalität hat gehandelt. Was immer du selbst tust, bedenke was du jetzt erfahren hast.

INE KLEINE CLIQUE?

n seiner Radio-Ansprache hat Hitler zugegeben, dass der
dens-Putsch von deutschen Offizieren organisiert worden
Göring nannte in seiner Ansprache die Männer hinter
Bewegung „eine kleine Clique von ehemaligen
eralen".

Hier sind die unbestreitbaren Tatsachen :
Hitler und Himmler haben die militärische
Leitung des Krieges gänzlich aus den Händen
der Berufsoffiziere genommen. Unter den von
Hitler abgesetzten Generalen sind :

Generalfeldmarschall Fedor v. Bock,
Generalfeldmarschall Walter v. Brauchitsch,
Generalfeldmarschall Ewald v. Kleist,
Generalfeldmarschall Wilhelm Ritter v. Leeb,
Generalfeldmarschall Wilhelm List,
Generalfeldmarschall Fritz Erich v. Manstein,
Generalfeldmarschall Gerd v. Rundstedt,
Generalfeldmarschall Erich v. Witzleben,
Generaloberst Ludwig Beck,
Generaloberst Freiherr v. Falkenhausen,
Generaloberst Fritz Fromm,
Generaloberst Franz Halder,
Generaloberst Erich Höppner,
Generaloberst Richard Ruoff,
Generaloberst Adolf Strauss.

Ist das eine „kleine Clique"? Sind sie „ge-
wissenlos"? Jedenfalls handelt es sich bei den
bestehenden Generalen um Wehrmachts-
Offiziere, die in militärischen Belangen anders
enken als die politische Führung. Die „kleine
lique" bestand darauf, dass Deutschland den
rieg sofort beendigen muss.

s ist klar, dass es in Deutschlan etzt nur mehr
Seiten gibt : Die Seite der Kriegs-verlängerer und
eite der Friedens-Beschleuniger.

FEST STEHT FOLGENDES :

1. Dass die deutsche Generalität am besten weiss, wie die militärische Lage ist.

2. Dass die deutsche Generalität zu der Einsicht gelangt ist, dass Deutschland den Krieg verloren hat.

3. Dass die deutsche Generalität daher verlangt hat, dass der Krieg beendet wird.

4. Dass die deutsche politische Führung nicht Frieden schliessen kann ohne unterzugehen.

5. Dass die deutsche Generalität, als ihrem Verlangen nicht entsprochen wurde, selbst handeln musste.

6. Dass die Friedensbewegung nicht von einer „kleinen Clique" stammte, sondern von erfahrenen Generalen.

DU WEISST JETZT BESCHEID :

Heute weisst du, was die deutsche Generalität in den letzten Wochen selbst erkennen musste : dass Deutschland die militärische Niederlage nicht mehr vermeiden kann. Und dass die politische Führung nicht gewillt ist, daraus die Konsequenz zu ziehen. Warum ? Weil sie weiss, dass das Kriegsende ihr eigenes Ende bedeutet.

WAS IST ZU TUN ?

DIE HEIMAT tut, was sie kann, um den Frieden zu beschleunigen. Trotz Gestapo, trotz Hinrichtungen und Massenrepressalien haben Deutschlands Arbeiter erkannt, dass die Räder der Kriegsmaschine nur durch Massen-Arbeitsverweigerung stillgelegt werden können.
DIE FRONT selbst hat oft Gelegenheit, den Frieden zu beschleunigen. 50 000 deutsche Soldaten weigerten sich, auf der Cherbourg-Halbinsel Selbstmord zu begehen. Im Osten ergab sich die gesamte 4. Armee in hoffnungsloser Lage auf Befehl von Generalleutnant Müller.

Letzten Endes liegt es aber an dir selbst, ob du für dich selbst Frieden schliesst oder dich in den Untergang des Systems mitreissen lässt. Dein Leben liegt in deiner eigenen Hand. Und mit ihm die Zukunft Deutschlands. Denn Deutschland wird dich nach dem Krieg brauchen.

Preis **20**

Druck und Verlag
DuMont Schauberg
22. Juni 194
Nummer 25 / 19. Ja

Kölnische
frierte Zeitung

Weitere
Aufnahmen von der
INVASION
in diesem
Heft

„Ein entsetzliches Abenteuer"

PK Aufnahme H-Kriegsberichte

nennt der Londoner „Daily Sketch" den Invasionskampf, in den die britisch-amerikanischen Truppen geschickt wurden. Hier warten die ersten Gefangenen, der Hölle entronnen.
(Zum unserem Bildbericht „Europa, den 6 Juni")

"Une terrible aventure" c'est ainsi que le 'Daily Sketch' de Londres designe l'invasion des troupes anglo-americaines. Échappés de cet enfer, les premiers prisonniers attendent leur d
Una aventura tremenda" es la fecha de la invasion anglo-americana, segun el 'Daily Sketch' de Londres. Los primeros prisioneros escapados del infierno esperando su inter

The photo of 6 Airborne Division prisoners in Caen confirmed their capture the indefatigable BMA (Beach Maintenance Area) Key Plan. Among them must have been some collaborators.

When I went back to the Hermanville Dump and got working on the top covers (camouflage netting), I suddenly caught sight of the mysterious blonde, leaning on the gate and watching our activities. In some ways security was strangely lax. I wondered what her fate would have been with the Germans had the roles been reversed. I cannot remember what the Intelligence Officer said when I asked why she was still at large. Civilian life in Hermanville did not seem to have been greatly disturbed by the momentous events which had lapped it on all sides. I met the Parish Priest and, with Fitzsimmons, attended Mass in the ancient church. I see from my diary that on D + 4 I was even able to get my laundry done by some kind soul in Hermanville.

On D + 5, 11 June, I slept very late, past midday, for there had been no chance for normal sleep for five nights. The situation around Caen had not progressed much, but the Airborne Bridgehead had held and consolidated. We clearly had the upper hand in the air. It was a time to relax, so I did.

The next day was spent with our sister unit, the Bucks (Oxford and Bucks Light Infantry), 6 Beach Group, working in support of the 3 Canadian Div to the west. Dump cover repair was the main activity. I had dinner with John Langdon, who commanded one of the Companies of the King's. He had moved into a small house along the road towards Ouistreham which had the unwarlike name Chalet Fleurie – which he adopted and put up wherever his Company HQ moved in the succeeding weeks.

This dinner was memorable – all fresh food and good wine – but it was interrupted by an air raid along the line of the beaches. My jeep was parked on the road verge, and I had mounted a captured machine-gun (MG34) for such an opportunity. The planes were flying quite low and their dark shapes could be seen against the sky. I was not at all adept at firing the MG 34 but I got it going. The rate of fire was exceeding fast (one could say excessively fast for some purposes) but I hoped I found the target with a round or two. However, there was no sign that any plane was hit in spite of a mass of anti-aircraft fire, in which the craft along the beaches joined. The landing craft had anti-aircraft guns – the LCIs had Oerlikons mounted near the bows – and when there were sniper scares in the beach houses they seized the chance to let loose. Unfortunately the shots sometimes passed over the roofs, and troops further inland who came under fire assumed this was from the enemy. A near panic rumour started thus one evening – that a German counter

159

attack had broken through to the beach and was advancing on our flank.

On 14 June I visited the Casino Strongpoint which had been taken by a Royal Marine Commando and the French Commando. The incident was featured in the film *The Longest Day* and, quite understandably, has been made much of by the French. When I visited the beaches 18 years later I noticed that this action had been publicised out of all proportion, but when one thinks what the British attitude would have been to being liberated by the French from the Germans I do not suppose we would have failed to over-emphasise the part played by a sole British Commando.

D + 2/3

Brother John's LCA's after damage on landing Queen

Capt Basil Spence and Sergeant Heath

There was a heavy coastal battery under construction beside the area where the demolished Casino had stood. Very crude dummy guns made of telegraph poles and junk had been put in the completed emplacements. Just behind them stood a curious tall concrete tower, the walls blank of any apertures or loopholes except at the top. There, facing out across the Channel, was a wide open slot designed to house a large rangefinder. It had received a direct hit dead centre above the opening in the Naval shelling.

To enter the Keep, as it was called, one had to follow a narrow passage below ground level and round a couple of corners, then through a heavy metal door which was covered from the angle in the passage by a loophole. This was closed by a heavy spherical metal plate through which a machine-gun was mounted. It would have been costly to try to capture the tower by assault and unnecessary, as it could no longer play an active role or threaten the Beach Group troops. It was believed that a small handful of Germans had sealed themselves inside. A light AA Bofors gun was sited nearby and, as several days passed uneventfully, the presence of Germans was almost forgotten. Then, quite unexpectedly, a German carrying a white flag led out a very considerable party of men to surrender to the astonished gun crew.

Tank obstacles. Casino Strongpoint

Ouistreham Strongpoint

Excavator flame-thrower and tanglefoot wire

Uncompleted battery

162

Ouistreham Strongpoint

The Keep with direct hit in centre of slit for range finder already in place (dummy Battery in foreground)

Heavy mobile anti tank gun in Casino bunker Roger Red

Later I foraged into the Keep. The Germans had made as disgusting a mess of the place as they could before leaving. It was completely black inside, windowless and smelling foul. I did, however, recover from the Keep a considerable length of intensely bright orange flourescent material which I imagine was intended for ground to air signalling. I also acquired some German knives, forks and spoons. The rangefinder had already been mounted, although the battery was incomplete, but its aperture offered a grandstand view of the invasion fleet, assembled a few thousand yards offshore. I suppose our captured Germans had been watching hopefully for its withdrawal or other signs of a German counter attack on the beach area – until they eventually began to run out of food and water and surrendered.

The Casino strongpoint was full of interesting features and I took several photographs. The beach widened near the Ouistreham corner, where the Canal joined the sea, and there was a flat sandy area with a few low sandhills and a wide variety of defensive obstacles, concrete gun postions and 'murderous devices'. One of these devices was a flame thrower. The cylinder was dug in with only its nozzle protruding a few inches above the sand, and it was camouflaged with sea grass. I traced the control wire (which would set this off electrically) back to a pill box with a wide view of the open beach which the assaulting troops must cross. The area in front of this flame thrower was covered with with a type of barbed wire known as tanglefoot, calculated to trap the legs and slow down the attack. When a satisfactorily large group of attackers had bunched up, the flame thrower would be fired.

This was a safe and simple investigation to make compared with one I undertook back in the 0880 Strongpoint. There we had discovered a small shelter dug into the side of a sandhill and opening on to the beach. It was made of pine logs and covered with sand and grass. Inside was a small tracked vehicle more like a toy than a real weapon. Its purpose was not at first known, but I crawled into this kind of kennel and, feeling around behind the back of the baby tank, I found some thin, brightly coloured electric cables. These I traced back to a control pill box to the rear, and there I found a switch device. Assuming that its purpose was to motivate and control the movement of the miniature tank, I then deduced that it must contain high explosive which could be detonated by remote control, presumably when the 'tank' had been moved into a concentration of assault vehicles or troops.

It seemed desirable to disarm such a large amount of high explosive nestling near the heart of the Beach Group HQ. To do this by the control switch, without knowing the correct procedure, was too risky – it might start moving or blow up, or both. So I decided simply to disconnect it and again crawled into the kennel with a jack knife open in my hand. I folded the coloured strands over the knife edge and was about to cut through them when some dim inner warning stopped me. I remembered something in my training about not cutting through all the wires of such systems at one, but separating them and cutting them individually. Then common sense returned. I crawled out backwards and did what I should have done in the first place – found the nearest Bomb Disposal Sapper and told him all. He had a look at the device and quietly informed me that if my knife blade had contacted the three wires at once the thing would have blown up.

These 'tanks' were regarded as rather a joke, and this one was later run out of its lair and caused much delight, being driven around, controlled invisibly from the pill box and later driven by with yelling men of the Beach Group sitting on top. They were called doodle bugs or beetle tanks, and they must have been a very recent addition to the defences. I believe the German name for them was Goliath. I had noticed some fine Mercedes staff cars being furtively driven on to landing craft, and wondered if it would be possible for me to smuggle a beetle tank home as a present for Simon! The pine trees used to construct the lairs for these Goliaths had come from a small wood visible in the air photographs and shown as existing in the Defence Overprint. The wood had, however, been felled by 6 June. In 1962, 18 years later I stayed overnight in the neighbourhood with my son Nicholas and daughter Clare, and the space where the wood had been was transformed into a caravan site.

15 June, D + 9. My diary says, 'Heavier shelling of Queen Beach. Five LST hit. Six killed. 50 wounded. Try frantically to get decoy out. Do one on small scale. Then try to get some sense into smoke which was silhouetting craft from enemy view 100 degrees. Get arm and finger burned, and get wet trying to keep smoke going.'

In our situation, with the eastern flank of the landing beaches ending a short distance east of the 0880 Strongpoint, there remained about 2,500 yards of unused beach on the enemy side, where an ideal opportunity presented itself for a decoy and also much more intelligent use of smoke. A glance at the map or air photograph shows clearly how the Germans had perfect observation of the Sword beaches. If they could be offered a juicy dummy target a little apart from the eastern end of the concentration, erected to seem to have beached overnight and complete with simulated fires, etc, it could hardly fail to concentrate the fire of the German batteries which were now receovered and shelling Queen Beach effectively.

Certainly the opportunity was there, and the high powered UK based camouflage resources should have been able quickly to supply what was required. It would have been so simple with all these resources, compared with the problem of conjuring up a railhead out of virtually nothing, miles from anywhere in the desert. Now, however, being a relatively junior officer with a Beach Group, I had to propose my plan to Sub-Area (Basil Spence), then to 1st Corps (Sam Black), then to 2 Army, and probably to 21 Army Group, all of whom had to be convinced. In the outcome the chance was missed.

There had been so little opportunity for camouflage subtlety in the hurly burly of the last nine days that I was feeling angry and frustrated. The instance of the smoke screen was a case of sheer ineptitude. Maybe it was something to do with Peter Wiggins having been wounded and shipped back to England, because the laying of the smoke screen for an offshore breeze was done quite mechanically, it was at times having the effect of actually silhouetting the offshore and beached ships. For one thing the line of cannisters was not positioned far enough to the east from the viewpoint of the artillery, shelling from east of the Orne and observed from that direction. On the other hand a dense blanket of smoke blowing out to sea from the Ouistreham Casino area would have been totally effective for as long as it was sustained.

No landing operations had been undertaken as far east as this after the D Day Commando landing. Admittedly it was vulnerable to the enemy coastal defence guns across the Orne, but they did not react to the movement of isolated figures. I was so frustrated by the inadequacy of the smoke screen that I moved some of the smoking cannisters over to where they would be of some use. No one seemed interested or eager to help. Eventually I decided to take one out to a beached craft which was in shallow water at low tide, and I waded out, hugging the burning cannister – which was quite cool at the bottom but could not be touched near the top. I climbed hurriedly over the stern hoping my activity was not interesting the distant German observers, and was suddenly faced by the ghastly sight of a closely packed mass of corpses, still pressed together as they had died on D Day. They had been washed by many tides, but the sight and stench was horrible – and I let go of the smoke cannister and fled.

16 June, D + 10. Diary notes: 'Press again for work on vehicle pits. Good progress. Recce to Canal with Basil and Beattie Pownall (Camouflage Officer with 6 Beach Group). Still some D Day bodies about. To Army to get backing for decoy scheme. Neither Basil nor Army were enthusiastic, but I pressed on.'

The next few days were wet and stormy, with a very high tide on the 19th, causing beach work to cease. 68 small craft were damaged in the storm, which would have been very serious if the Mulberry Harbour had not been well advanced along the coast to the west at Arromanches. I photographed the landing craft, including a number of damaged LCAs, some of which were from Broadsword, by brother John's flotilla.

On 21 and 22 June (D + 15 and + 16) there was heavy shelling and mortaring of Ouistreham docks and of the beach 100 yards or so beyond our dugout. One ammunition coaster was hit.

The Ouistreham Docks Screen was occupying a great deal of my time at this point. The idea behind the scheme is best understood by reading the document *Proposed Screening Schemes at Ouistreham Docks* in conjuction with the air photographs and ground photographs. In retrospect it seems very optimistic to have hoped to use the dock facilities at the northern end of the Caen Canal – however much this would have helped the all important speed of off-loading and turn round of ships. From the east the area was already partly screened from ground observation by the group of buildings around the lighthouse, and to screen off the gaps was simple enough. The decoy area seemed a relatively easily produced deception to keep the German spotters and gunners busy. However, the German reaction was such that any activity was immediately shelled with such accuracy by 88 mm guns that work had to be abandoned.

The 88 mm gun was one of the most feared and respected German weapons – by tanks far more than aircraft. The gun, whose flash we had seen coming from a concrete casemate in the sandhills across the flat Orne estuary, was thought to be a Naval quick-firing gun. Since its exact position could be seen and indicated, it seemed worthwhile to try to arrange for some effective reply. At this point there was no British artillery positioned to return fire. Basil Spence and I made a very detailed drawing of the area of sandhills and the particular loophole, after close examination through binoculars, and took it to BRA (Brigadier Royal Artillery) at 3 British Div. With it we took the most accurate six point map reference we could calculate – and left it to him to react.

PROPOSED SCREENING SCHEME FOR QUISTREHAM DOCKS.

1. INFORMATION. Ref Sketch Plan Appendix "A".
It may be necessary to dock coasters in the QUISTREHAM LOCK AND This BASIN is within range of enemy heavy mortar in the R.... VILLE PLAGE and within shelling range of heavier enemy b.. further ...
Enemy has restricted observation of L... AREA from his O.P's probabl sufficient to observe exact fall of fire on the corner ... off loading area.

2. INTENTION. (a) To ... ENEMY OBSERVATION ... and protect LOCK G...
(b) TO LIMIT THIS OBSERVATION ... to areas where no work is to take place.

3. METHOD. (a) To achieve A it is intended to erect a Vertical Screen in a position a shown on Appendix "A" (Blue line).
The actual berth for coaster discharge is already largely screened from enemy observation by buildings etc & only gaps & a prolongation by scr will be necessary. The lowering of high spars & masts on coast rs ma be necessary & whenever possible entry & exits should be made in darkness or behind smoke.

(b) To achieve "B" a further obvious screen is to be erected in position a shown in Appendix "A" (Red line).
This will deny enemy observation of a portion of basin where loading o take place & where craft already lie - with damaged cranes etc alongsi Enemy interest from ground and air view would have to be maintained by movement of masts & crane tops - smoke etc above decoy screen.

+ Centres of Real and Decoy screen are about 400 yds apart. This shoul sufficient deflection to reduce ... considerably the effect of shelling & mortaring of real work area.

4. REQUIREMENTS. (a) **Material.**
Nets garnished	....	nos. 100
S.W.R. (Balloon Cable)	....	ft 1400
Pulleys light	....	nos. 25
Holdfasts ord pattern	....	" 40
Pickets, angle iron 4'	....	" 250
String	....	balls 2.

NOTE:- Upright supports already exist in the form of telegraph poles & concrete pylons etc - but certain additions will be necessary - avail able from local salvage.

(b) **Labour.**
20 Pioneers in two parties of 10 each. One NCO required for each party After completion - permanent party of 10 Pioneers for maintenance.

(c) **Transport**
One three ton truck for one to two days.

(d) **Time.**
Two days to construct screen as from the time all materials are to hand

(e) **Devices**
Dummy DUKWs (available)
Cranes etc (from local salvage)

5. SECURITY. As close observation of area can be obtained by civilians in parts of QUISTREHAM a prohibited area must be established. See Appx "A" (hatche area)

6. A.A. DEF. Screens will inevitably reduce field of fire for LAA but it is presumed that the danger from mortar and shell fire overrides that from enemy A/

F.B.Hydee.
Capt. R.E,
S.C. Cam,
5 Beach Group.

Ouistreham dock screening and decoy scheme

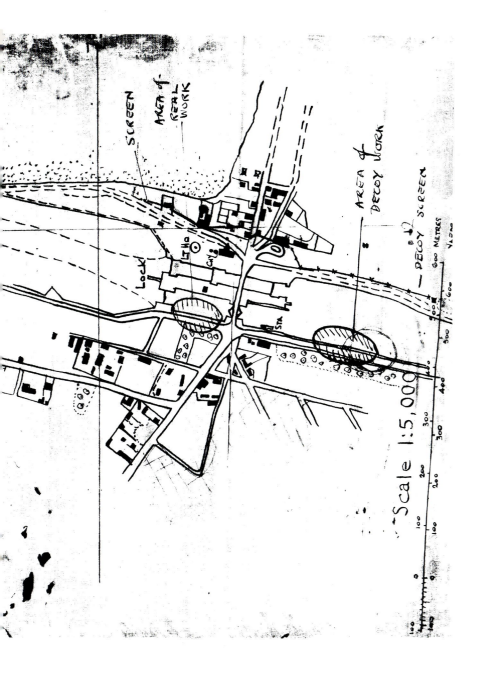

SCREEN

AREA OF
REAL
WORK

AREA OF
DECOY WORK

DECOY SCREEN

600 METRES
YARDS

500

400

300
300

200
200

100
100

0

Scale 1:5,000

Lock

LtHo

Ch

STA

In no time orders were given for a self-propelled gun (a Priest), which carried a 25 pounder) to proceed to the Canal Bridge area and to report to me. This calibre of gun should have been more than enough at such short range to deal with the offending German position. I had been active, while waiting for it to arrive, in preparing a distraction for the Germans when the Priest opened up. A narrow spit of land projected northwards from the large warehouse building beside the lighthouse, on the eastern Canal bank. This was thick with defences, maching-gun turrets, communication trenches and wire.

I took some German stick grenades and tied them to the barbed wire fence on the side facing the German pill box, then unscrewed the caps on the handles and tied a line of string from each pull-string in the grenades to a control position in the trench. There were two groups, and two firing positions. Basil manned one and I the other. When the Priest arrived near the Canal Bridge it was halted out of sight while the Gunner Officer was shown exactly where the loophole target was. He then chose a position for the shoot. This involved the Priest crossing the Canal Bridge, turning left behind the group of lighthouse buildings, and halting in a gap where it had a view of the target. The target also had a view of the self-propelled gun and had possibly been warned by the sound of its approach. I hoped that, when it opened up, the other flashes from the grenades would initially confuse the Germans as to the exact source of the attack.

The Priest lumbered into position and fired its first round, while Basil and I also let off some grenades. Before a second round could be fired, the German gun opened up in reply within a matter of seconds, and although the Priest got off some 12 rounds, the response was so rapid and accurate that it backed away hurriedly behind the building, and our little excitement was over. The gun layer was convinced he had seen a shot enter the aperture, but as the German gun had continued firing this was doubtful. Some weeks later, after we have advanced, I was able to seek out this German pill box and look at the evidence.

On 24 June, D + 18, the Beach Group HQ moved into a house in Lion-sur-Mer, further west along the coast. It was called *Deux Soeurs*, and was an old building which had belonged to a family with considerable taste, plus it had a well furnished garden. A sharp engagement between the Marine Commandos and occupying Germans had been fought here, and there were graves of both in the garden.

27 June, D + 21. My diary reports continuing shelling, which in

a way vindicated the setting up of the screen. I had gone across the Caen Canal and the River Orne to the 6 Airborne Bridgehead, then up to its northern extremity near a village called Sallenelles, held by No 4 Special Service (RM Commando). They took me to a very exposed observation post within sight of the Merville Battery – which was still held by the Germans although put out of action on D Day by the Airborne landings. From here I could gain an idea of the enemy view of the lighthouse area, where we were erecting the screen. I must have learned something significant, for according to my diary I worked through the night until 0430. Efforts to work on the high 15 ft netting in daylight had drawn machine-gun fire, so we had to work at night.

1 July, D + 26, was marked by our Guest Night Dinner, when the guests were the Company Commanders. I have kept the menu of this dinner, with the Company Commanders' signatures, though some were missing and presumably on duty, notably Appleton, Denton and Langdon. I was Duty Officer that night and left the party early to take up my post in the watch room at *Deux Souers*. This was a large, rather lovely room with french windows opening on to the garden. Naturally all curtains were drawn for blackout purposes. I started pacing up and down the room to keep awake, and at about 1 am I heard the drone of a plane getting louder and then beginning to recede. I had just reached the window and was in no way alarmed by the plane, when the blast from a huge explosion nearly knocked me over.

The blackout curtains had been blown down but had nevertheless served to hold up the flying glass from the shattered windows. The lights had gone out. I had a torch and was able to find my way out into the garden, for I was convinced that the explosion had been, if not in the room, at least just outside in the garden, but I could see no evidence of this. In fact it had been at least 300 yards away. A very large landmine had been parachuted down (hence the delay in the detonation) and had landed near the church. There were 15 civilian casualties, which number included the Mayor (a Resistance fighter), the doctor and other notables.

The next day a security drive was laid on, and considering the horror of losing nearly all the village notables in the previous night's disaster, the methodical search of every house was accepted very gracefully by the locals. Neverthless, we were made to feel very foolish by some of the households, who looked dramatically under tables and opened small cupboards – in fact, generally mocked our search. It was perhaps fortunate that during the next day a real live German was indeed found. He had been hiding in a small loft above a garage – behind one of the long lines of seaside villas between Lion-sur-Mer and the 0880 Strongpoint. He had come down from his cramped roost to have a shave, and although the house was quite empty of troops he was spotted by a member of the Beach Group.

The new Beach Group Commander – a Colonel from the Irish Battalion of the King's Liverpools, complete with corbeen and cock's feather headgear – had the German paraded rather ostentatiously round Lion-sur-Mer so that our sudden house search would be better justified. I do not believe the German had been taking any active part in the war for the last three weeks, but to have existed for so long undiscovered was a considerable feat.

On 3 July, D + 27, I heard that I was wanted for 6 Airborne Division. The news was brought to me by John Hutton, who had been on the camouflage course with me at Larkhill and was now administering the 21 Army Group Camouflage Pool of Officers. John and I were both, in the post-war years, to collaborate with Basil Spence in Coventry Cathedral – John in the designing and engraving of the Great West Window and I in the *ciment-fondu* relief of the Angel with a Chalice and the sleeping disciples in the Chapel of Christ in Gethsamane. And here we were, all three of us, in a very different role.

Three days later I left to join another outfit. A lot had happened since I joined King's 120 days ago at Loch-na-bo – the Leap Year Exercise, the tea-less trek to Emsworth, the false alarms and waiting, Lena Horne singing *Honeysuckle Rose*, the Channel crossing and all the adventures and excitements from D Day onwards in the concentrated area of Queen White. I had made good friends with many people in the King's, and now I had to start all over again – such is the lot of the Pool Officer.

11

6 Airborne Division (to which I was posted on D + 30) was a very closed family circle and they thought little of non-airborne outsiders, so I approached my new posting with some misgivings. At the outset my worst fears were confirmed, but the fact that I had been near their Bridgehead early D Day morning helped to break the ice. One of them even confessed that he would, after seeing the Defence Overprint for the Ouistreham area, have preferred to parachute in beyond rather than land on the beaches. I was attached to the CRE of the Division (Col Loman) and was to Mess with him and the Royal Engineers Intelligence Officer, Lt Leslie Shand.

My job was to try to organise that dumps in a large area of the countryside were disposed for quick dispersal as widely and as soon as possible, and I had to make sure that the stores were placed in such a way that they were not obvious – that, according to one's knowledge of air reconnaissance they would look part of the countryside.

The area occupied by 6 Airborne Div from the time of the capture of Pegasus Bridge (before dawn on 6 June) to the general advance in August was, in addition to being plagued by mosquitoes, extremely unpleasant in the Bois de Bavent area, shared with the Germans, where dead bloated and stinking horses and cattle caused a malevolent atmosphere.

6 Div HQ was spread under the small escarpment which ran north-south, parallel with the Orne and about 500 yards east of it – a little under a mile north of the east-west road which crossed both river and canal at the now famous Pegasus Bridge. Some of the HQ offices were located in tunnels burrowed into the rocky cliff face and were fitted with a ventilation system. They had moved there from nearby Ranville. The landing and dropping zone of D Day and after stretched across the flat fields a little to the east.

Sgt Heath, Fitzsimmons and I tried for a night or two to sleep in a ventilation shaft where we would be safe from shelling, but the whole area was overrun by hordes of mosquitoes and this ventilation shaft seemed to have a special attraction for them. We soon abandoned it. In the water meadows between the cliff and the river there were a number of abandoned slit trenches, and we adopted these for our sleeping quarters. I worked hard to make mine insect-proof with fine mesh netting, which I could lay aside to climb in and replace once inside. There were, however, lots of other insects – spiders and beetles, which seemed to arrive from below the net and I had some really poor nights' sleep. It was too hot to remain tightly covered, face and all, in one's sleeping bag.

The other hazard was that this stretch of water meadow was, from the German gunners' point of view, just short of a strange isolated bridge over the river. This bridge was no more than a connection between two tracks running through the fields and along the canal and river banks. There was no complementary bridge over the canal and perhaps for this reason it played no part in the action. It did seem, however, that the German artillery was having a go at it from time to time, and we were uncomfortably near.

One day when I was in the field a shell, making all the expected whooshing noises shells are supposed to make, landed in the field, grooved up a lot of turf and bounced on towards the river. I found it a 100 yards away in the next meadow, lying unexploded on the surface. It was detonated by the Sappers.

I now had to get to know the Bridgehead area, the Commanders of the Units, and the need for camouflage. On 10 July I saw the G1, who suggested concentration on sniper concealment and decoys. This was very satisfactory from my point of view – a positive activity which the fighting troops had requested, rather than a case of having to persuade the uninterested, as had happened too often in the past.

Air photographs covered most of the Bridgehead, which was held until the advance started in August. The landscape was cut up into small irregular fields, separated by thick hedges and dotted about with many areas of woodland. I could visit the various Brigade HQs in the jeep, but it was very easy to proceed too far down the sheltered lanes and into enemy territory, for there was sometimes nothing on the road to indicate that this was 'far enough'.

Altogether the short term situation was in sharp contrast to the elaborately prepared long term set up which we had found in the beach defences. Here we were fighting a strange kind of war, where camouflage had suddenly reverted to what we had first been taught. Most of the Instructors in Britain were, in fact, still training people to disguise themselves in fluid situations as a hedge or a tree or a brick wall (in the Middle East, of course, there was no such opportunity!) But this had now become a sniper war – static, with no attempt to advance. We were waiting for the breakthrough further west, which eventually happened.

At Airborne Div I had to do strictly practical instruction. In fact, it was a case of instructing the troops in situ; it was necessary to go up to a unit which was, for instance, actually holding a bridge. You never knew how close you were to the Germans, and a hedgerow would, over its length, be shared by Germans at one end and the Airborne people at the other. 6 Airborne Div had five brigades under their command, and a Marine Commando at the coast end.

On 11 July the Airborne Div G1 wanted, or thought he wanted, a very realistic figure for the sniper decoys he was suggesting. He told me of an artist (a potter actually) whose factory was more or less in the front line near Le Mesnil. I had been astonished at the number of ceramic cats stalking ceramic birds on the roofs of the villas at La Brèche, Riva Bella and Lion-sur-Mer. The answer lay in the Le Mesnil pottery.

The G1 saw Monsieur Dupont as a natural dummy modeller, and the potter himself told me that he had been ordered by the Germans to make a number of circular pottery containers for Teller mines; these were thickly sewn on the beaches, with many more mounted on top of the stakes set in rows to obstruct landing craft. I had tried out my previous sniper's rifle on these, hoping they would blow up, but without much success. The point of Monsieur Dupont's mine cases was presumably to protect them from the sea water, and he proudly described how he had concocted a clay body which, although when baked seemed strong enough, would quite rapidly dissolve in the sea water. He was unable to help with the snipers, but he told me to contact a French sculptor in Caen.

I had not been right into Caen since my holiday in the 1930s with my brother David, when we had enjoyed some good meals at Chez Alcide. The speciality was Tripe à la Mode de Caen. The northern sector had been blanketed by thousand-bomber raids, and as we drove in the road completely disappeared in rubble so that we had to scramble forward on foot. I remember meeting a solitary Frenchman and asking for directions to the sculptor. He looked at me in astonishment and began to cry. The whole sector had been obliterated by the Allied bombing and he, himself, had lost his entire family. In spite of this terrible personal tragedy he tried to be helpful and friendly. The full horror of it all was that the bombing had not had the desired effect – rather the opposite, for the rubble into which the Germans had rapidly moved when the bombing ceased had proved easier to defend than the undamaged streets would have been. In the event I never found the sculptor.

The next day the failings of the realistic sniper idea had become clear and the plan was dropped. No good sniper would show his face clearly enough for realism of modelling to count. We found, Sgt Heath and I, a more appropriate solution. I had a word with the CRE at Div HQ and he said, 'You had better go out and visit the various brigades and ask them what they need.'

In all cases the answer was the same. The Brigade Commanders' reaction was, could I concoct a good disguise for our snipers which the men could construct themselves; also, could I devise a way of drawing enemy sniper fire on to a dummy, so that the angle of penetration of the shot could be noted, for we were losing a lot of men among the hedges. When a man has been shot it is hard to know where the shot has come from, whereas clues could be gained from an in or out mark on, say, a cardboard tube. I produced for them dummy figures which were made up from available ammunition cartons, with an Airborne helmet on top; you could not see what was inside – it looked like a man using an Airborne camouflage smock. These dummies had to be rather carefully constructed and placed so that they could be raised to draw fire and pulled down again for examination.

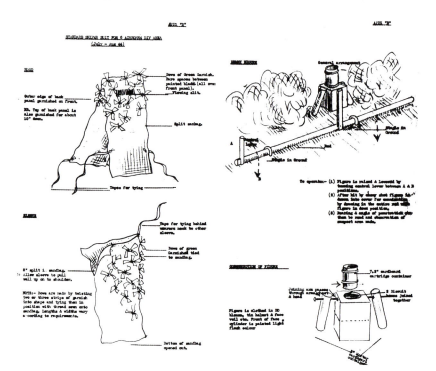

12 July. Diary notes, 'Make sniper hoods at Field Park in morning. To 5 Parachute Brigade and 13 Parachute Battalion in afternoon. Try out sniper suit in most dangerous positions. No response from Germans.'

Hard work was put into preparing and delivering sniper hoods and painting 70 yards of hessian for 13 Battalion screens. Then, on 15 July, there was a concerted effort by 21 Army Camouflage Pool. We were all summoned from our units to rendezvous at Army HQ for detailed instructions. The operation (to take place in darkness) involved a switch of armour from west to east – carefully planned with Camouflage Officers attached to all the units involved in the move.

This operation, code named Goodwood, is one of the rare occasions when the Pool Camouflage Officers were together. In operation Goodwood three armoured divisions, the Guards, the Seventh and Eleventh, were to be switched secretly from much further west (Camilly). A large number of tanks were switched some 15 miles after dark, and each tank had to be guided into its selected 'harbour' area and concealed before dawn.

I photographed my unit, the 3 RTR, as they appeared in the morning, very well absorbed into the hedges all round a large field, but I doubt if a good air photograph interpreter would not have

Sniper suit, lower half uncamouflaged

177

spotted them as lumps in the hedge pattern and from careless tracks. After dark they moved on to the canal and Orne crossings and the attack was launched southwards after dawn from an area round Ranville, which we hoped the Germans had thought was clear of armoured units.

The attack was preceded by an Oboe, the code name for a thousand-bomber raid. I sketched my impression of this. The slice of country where the tanks were to advance was pulverised, a pinkish pall of smoke and dust rising right across the distant landscape. One could not help wondering what was happening to the villages in its path. Bourgébus was one. Although it seemed that a thousand bombers and hundreds of tanks would surely strike through to Caen and beyond, the attack was only partially successful. I finished the day with a visit to the relative comfort of HQ Beach Group in Lion-sur-Mer.

I had entrusted my precious D Day photographs to Sam Black, the Camouflage Officer at No 1 Corps HQ, the only place where the processing could be done. However, before the films were dry the Corps had to move and the result is very evident in the photographs.

Life was now back to normal with 6 Airborne Div. The Colonels commanding the Parachute Battalions and Commandos were most impressive characters, tough and lively and liberally decorated with MCs and DSOs. The procedure in trying to sell them the sniper hoods was to arrange to call the HQ, usually in some deserted house, and ask the Colonel and HQ staff to hide their eyes for a few minutes. Sgt Heath would then put on a hood and quickly take cover among some suitable bushes or the lower branches of trees in the back garden, generally only a few yards away. They would then emerge from the house and look for 'the sniper'.

The disguise was remarkably effective. If the mixture of colours, greens and browns in the garnishing of the sandbag smock was near that of the undergrowth it was somewhat impossible, even at very close range, to see where the figure was. We had given this demonstration of sniper concealment to the COs with equal success, so we started giving instruction, showing exactly how to make the camouflage which they must, of course, adapt to their own circumstances.

24 July was a sad day. I had accompanied the CRE, Col Loman, Leslie Shand and Col Tew, the Chief Signals Officer of the Division on a visit by jeep to the captured Colombelles Steel Works four days before. Col Loman had agreed that we should have dinner at the Grand Hotel, Lion, and I went to order a table. On my return I

found that Leslie Shand was killed, having touched off a mine on a reconnaissance, and the CRE was badly injured.

My diary records, 'To Leslie's funeral and back to cancel dinner. Bombing at night.' I had struck up quite a friendship with young Shand. Some days before I had brought back a large bunch of wild cyclamen which I had found in a small wood near the river and had put them in a mug on our RE Mess table. He had, I think, been rather unsure how the CRE would react to this, but commented, after the meal, how pretty they were. We had moved around together and the suddenness of the whole event was shocking; and to attend his burial in the little graveyard by Ranville Church on the very same day seemed too sudden and final. This graveyard was rapidly filling with casualties from both the Airborne Division and the Highland Division who had replaced them in some sectors.

After this it was dull and rather sad, with two of our Mess of four gone. Maj Waters took over as CRE from Col Loman. Sniper hood demonstrations occupied the rest of July and there was a farewell dinner for 5 King's Regiment in Caen on their disbandment as a battalion – at which Ernie Quinn and I sang a parody of *Lilli Marlene* which I had recently concocted.

I continued working on sniper concealment, but one of the snags about these front line demonstrations was that sometimes a sudden mortar barrage would start and everyone would vanish into slit trenches, while Sgt Heath and I would be left high and dry – as when the music stops in Musical Chairs. At one point Heath expressed the view that he thought we were being foolhardy. I said I thought the whole business was inclined to be somewhat foolhardy, but I knew what he meant.

The Canadian Commando were in a very densely wooded part of the front line and were worried by the success of a German sniper who had claimed a number of victims. They were unable to get a fix on his positon – therefore I went away to make a fixing device but shortly after this, the whole front began to move forward, so it was not fully tested.

On 17 August my diary says, 'To Dives for CRE. Thousands of mine cases in hedges. Dead horses. To Bavent and on to Bricqueville.' By 21 August I was recording 'Very wet and miserable. Mosquitoes unbearable. To Dives-sur-Mer with Belgian armoured car. To recce road from Troarn-Dozulé road. Not mined. Dives in good shape. Few civilians but some from Houlgate.'

22 August, 'Not notified of changed time for new HQ move. Nice country beyond Dozulé. More people about. HQ RE arrive.

German and British tanks Bois de Bavent

Burned out German tank

Calkined driver of
German tank

Note lucky horseshoe
Tank confrontation in the Bois de Bavent

The jeep Psyche. Sgnt Heath and Fitzsimmons and Steven Sykes

Meeting with M and Mme Chorin just elected Mayor of Villers Sur Mer

Go off at once on job for CRE re BR Column. Meet it. Many salutations, Calvados, cider, no food. To Beuzeville, where collaborators are being put inside. To Pont l'Evèque. Shelling. Fires. Division moved again. Pitch tents, etc new site. Hardly any mosquitoes.

23 August, 'To Villers-sur-Mer. Very undamaged. Invited to lunch by charming couple (new Mayor). To Houlgate and Dives. Recce factory for materials. Warm welcome, cider etc.'

Such brief diary comments hardly express the great feeling of exultation during this advance. We had been stuck in the damp mosquito-infested country, and such places as Troarn had only been names in Intelligence reports; the other places, Houlgate and Villers on the coast, and Dozulé and Beuzeville were just names of unattainable places beyond the horizon.

The advance was quite rapid and mainly along two roads – on the coast road by the Belgian Brigade which had come under command of 6 Division, and the Airborne troops eastwards along the inland road through Beuzeville, towards Pont l'Evèque eastwards on the river Touques. There were numerous minor roads and country lanes connecting these main parallel lines of advance, and they had to be checked for enemy pockets of resistance or stragglers.

While following one of these quiet lanes we came upon a French countrywoman who had, on seeing the military vehicles approaching, thrown herself into the ditch in an effort to disappear. We stopped the jeep level with where she had vanished, and presently a ruddy country face cautiously showed itself. Her expression of alarm turned to puzzlement as she scrutinised us, our uniforms and our jeep, and suddenly she leapt out of the ditch with a yell of delight. I had dismounted and was clasped in a violent hug as she exclaimed, again and again through tears of joy, 'Ah – mes braves gens – mes braves gens!'

I had another very comical, but nonetheless touching, meeting near Pont l'Evèque. The Germans had set parts of the town on fire and demolished the bridge. I was sent by CRE to investigate the rumours of a ford up river. To find this I followed a very quiet lane for some time and presently, round a sharp corner, I encountered a complete French family, Papa, Mama, and a number of children. The father, when he realised he was at last face to face with the 'liberators', strode up to me and, snatching a huge bottle from under his coat, he whipped off the stopper and poured and sprinkled it all over me, crying, 'Zee Chermans, haff not!' It transpired that he was a barber and perfume shop owner. Before his business went up in flames he had salvaged one huge bottle of Eau de Cologne – and was putting it to the best use he could think of. Apart from being temporarily blinded by the burning spirit, I felt very agreeably welcomed.

On our arrival in Beuzeville on 22 August I photographed the scene. The place had only just been liberated and there was much excitement in the street. The photograph shows the former German Kommandantur with crowds in front and one Frenchman wearing what looks like a cuirassier or fireman's helmet. Resistance armbands and V signs are evident. I believe the collaborateurs were being paraded in front of the Kommandantur when the photograph was taken.

On 24 August my diary records 'many haircuts' in Deauville. These haircuts refer to the local collaboratrices whose heads had been shaved. They were at this stage all cooped up together in some cellars in Deauville and we were pressed to inspect them by the excited French people. They were a rather good looking bunch in spite of their shaven heads, looking sullen and apprehensive of their fate. In fact the punishment for their behaviour towards the Germans, from whom they had received many favours, was really quite apt and humane. By the time their hair grew the bitterness and resentment would have subsided and they could hope to slip back to normal relationships. Many of them tried to conceal their reputations by hitching lifts on Allied convoys in order to leave the area where their activities were known.

28 August, 'Division goes into rest.' This meant that once again I had to be allotted to a new formation, although there was some question of my being invited to return to England with Airborne Division. I had been with them for two months.

30 August, 'Saw John Hutton at Gacé. No job.' I was 30 years old on this day. Army Group was still near Bayeux. 2 Army HQ at Gacé was about a 70-mile run from Bayeux. The Caen-Falaise road was littered with burned out German transport and tanks, and along the minor road to Trun and on to Gacé there was even more stark evidence of how the Allied Forces had harassed and destroyed the crowded German columns retreating south-eastwards towards Paris in the last few days.

The return to 6 Division without a job was rather an anticlimax. The road from Gacé to Trouville led through Lisieux which, as a vital communications centre, had received a terrible pounding. A few idle days brought compensations and I remember going to an Anglo-French entertainment at a pleasant 19th-century seaside theatre in the Trouville Casino. Then, on 2 September, the first

1. On the 6th June we came to Normandy. We siezed the bridges, the Le Plein - Le Mesnil high ground and the Ranville areas.

2. What we siezed we held.

3. For two months we sat on the defensive while General Montgomery's great play unfolded itself.

4. On the 17th Aug we started a grim pursuit. Since then we have advanced 40 miles. This is an average of 7,000 yds a day as the crow flies, as the troops have had to march it has been half as far again.

5. We have fought and beaten the enemy at CABOURG, GOUSTRANVILLE, DOZULE, RYANVILLE, ANGERAULT, PONT L'EVEQUE, EQUAINVILLE, and BEUZEVILLE.

6. In this fighting we have lost many good friends. We have, all of us, at times been tired out and weary.

7. We have fought side by side with our gallant allies, the Belgians and the Dutch. The Green and the Red Berets have fought as one.

150 and 191 Field Regiments and 60 Heavy Anti Aircraft Regiment have supported us splendidly, effectively and loyally.

8. I congratulate you on your great achievements: on your stamina, on your skill and on your grand grim determination.

9. The motto of the 6th British Airborne Division is "GO TO IT". You have gone to it and right splendidly you have done it.

Richard N. Gale

Major-General,
Commanding 6th British Airborne Division.

2/3 Aug 44

---

party of 6 Airborne left for the UK via Arromanches, and I started to paint my impressions of the events in the three months since D Day.

3 September, the diary reads, 'Pack. Leave 10.30. Meet Hutton Lisieux road. To Sallenelles. Inspect old pill box across Orne. To Lion. Supper with Langdon and Denton.' The old pill box was the German gun position which we had tried to put out of action by the Priest tank, and Heath and I were anxious to inspect it and check our success. If the claim of the Priest crew was correct we would find evidence inside the pill box. It was quite difficult to be sure we had come to the right one as we could not check it from the lighthouse area, but after carefully looking around from the beach at low tide (keeping keen eyes for the mines) we felt we had found the right one. There was no evidence of damage inside, but we did discover a gun barrel – badly grooved on one side. This could only have been a direct hit coming in through the loophole and must have come from our Priest. What was hard to explain was the speed with which the spare barrel had been brought into action.

12

On 5 September I visited RAF and Army Group Intelligence to learn the locations of Buzz Bomb sites, for my next task was a review of concealment of the V1 and V2 Bomb sites which had been overrun by the advance into Belgium. My diary also recorded – of less national interest – 'mushrooming'. Mushrooming was my spare time activity and became a real passion. I managed to find a steady supply throughout the autumn and usually handed them into some small French or Belgian country restaurant, then returned to a really delicious evening meal.

I was ordered, on 6 September, to take some urgent Top Secret material from 21 Army Group, still in Bayeux, to the Advanced HQ now in Brussels. This fitted in with the V weapon site reconnaissance, and was a memorable journey marred by four flat tyres between Rouen and Amiens. The route was Amiens, Albert, Cambrai and Mons. My diary records, 'Belgians very enthusiastic. Given beer, butter and apples. Arrive Brussels 1330. Very cold. Bad weather all day. Incredible atmosphere in Brussels.'

This sudden sprint of 300 miles (with Heath and Fitzsimmons) was a heady experience after so much stagnation and limited movement in Normandy. To be in Amiens again was coming full circle, but I did not see the old Air Component Airfield of 1940. As we motored east we came through many of the battlegrounds and military cemeteries of the 1914-18 War. The Belgians in Mons did not yet seem to have got bored with British and American convoys, and I tried to photograph the crowds in the streets from the moving jeep. If the car halted we were at once showered with all kinds of bouquets and fruit, so we tried to keep moving, but even then gifts kept landing in the jeep. Having delivered the Top Secret packet to R Force we were directed to billet in the Grand Hotel, which had been taken over by the Army.

In Brussels the atmosphere was one of continuous carnival. The liberation had just been completed and the rejoicing had not flagged. From my hotel window I photographed the people who were still standing about in the street, waiting to grab anyone in khaki. As soon as I went out I was forcibly gathered into a long chain of young people dancing along the road. The leader, a girl, greeted me with 'Hello, boy!' – and that was it. I was adopted.

Bayeux, Bruxelles 6th September 1944

Sgt Heath

Fitzsimmons and Steven Sykes

Greeted in Belgium

187

Mons

Bruxelles 'Liberation'

We went to a large café, the Café Corso, where we sat and talked and drank. People were getting up and singing songs to the accompaniment of a small orchestra – Emile Deltour et son Orchestre. I was sufficiently carried away to get up and sing my version of *Lilli Marlene*. I told the orchestra leader, Emile Deltour, what the song was to be and, looking rather hesitant, he struck up the accompaniment, a trumpet call which preceded the refrain. The people in the café also glanced at each other doubtfully, wondering why, at this moment of all moments, they

188

Lilli Marlene

Before I sing this song to you
I'd better just explain
We stole it from the Afrika Corps,
it's called Lilli Marlene
And every night from Deutschlandsender
She would croon it soft and tender-
-ly to make them dream of home
In too much lebensraum.

In 1941 to Africa there came
A very cunning Hun
Von Rommel was his name.
He started very well and strong but oh!
He couldn't stay – he had to go
He left for Italy in 1943.

Now Fortress Europa's strong
And it can never fall
Since Rommel passed along
The great Atlantikwall.
It's full of 'Achtung Minen' boo-by trappen
Flamen-werfen secret mappen
And lovely lady snipers
Concealed in every room.

In 1944 it won't be any joke
We've such a lot in store
Fur das Deutsches Herrenfolk.
We've got to make our journey home
Via Berlin, Tokyo, Rome
Those of us left alive
    In 1945.

were being subjected to a popular German war song, but as the words came over they soon began to smile and applaud. I had to do one encore and then another. This was followed by an 'all together now' of *Tipperary*, the song which was heard just about non-stop over these jubilant days, and which clearly had been cherished by the Belgians as some kind of anthem of hope and confidence that the days of the German occupation would end and Tommies would return.

When I sat down after my unexpected performance I was approached by the band leader who told me, in broken English, that he had two identities – Emile Deltour et son Orchestre and also Eddie Tower and his Band, and he would like to have a copy of the words so that the band could perform the number. I tried to explain the subtleties of the parody without much success, and then, as he suggested making a gramophone recording, I offered to sing it myself. He was delighted, gave me his card, and I agreed to contact him. He explained that the recording would be made at the Decca Studios in a suburb of Brussels, but that the power shortage had restricted recording session to Saturdays only.

The next day, when I came into the foyer of the Hotel I found a group of my friends of the previous evening waiting for me. They wanted me to come to Polivox, a commercial recording studio, to sing *Lilli Marlene* and, of course, *Tipperary*. The booking had been made and they would not take no for an answer. At that point I noticed a somewhat sour-looking Colonel listening to the arrangements, and I felt a foreboding of trouble. I was waiting for my next orders, but meantime I made the record.

The session at Polivox was quite exhausting, as I seemed to have no breath and a considerable hangover. However, with the help of a very spirited piano accompaniment from Denis Maloens and, as they later inscribed the record, La Bande qui Chantait Faux, both *Lilli Marlene* and *Tipperary* were made safe for posterity. I returned to the hotel alone, having explained the problem of the disapproving Colonel.

Swanning was a term coined to describe the voluntary movement made by the Forces outside strict military requirements. It could represent marking time or a more positive case of rubber necking, the term for sightseeing. (Some cynic had renamed the Army Group Pool of Camouflage Officers 'Swan Lake'.) The mood of the Bruxelloises made such a prospect both inviting and difficult to avoid, and the Colonel was, no doubt, bent on stamping it out wherever his suspicions were aroused – and he certainly saw me swanning. Although, as yet, I had no orders to go elsewhere, I thought it wise to move away from Brussels.

When I informed Sgt Heath that we were about to leave he told me, rather sheepishly, that Fitzsimmons was not around. He had been adopted by a Belgian family the previous evening. However, Heath was able to run him to earth and we got away before the angry Colonel could strike. We went to 2 Army HQ which was some miles back, west of Brussels.

On 9 September I suddenly realised that the day was Saturday, the only recording day at Decca, and decided to take a chance and turn up at the Studios. Sure enough Emile (or Eddie) was there with his band, and after a brief discussion we got down to it. Each time something seemed to go wrong – not much, but enough to call for a further attempt, and all the time my lungs seemed to be seizing up. Heath was called in to fill out before the last verse with a whistled refrain, but he was not very adept and instead of being able to get my breath back I had to whistle too.

All seemed to be sorted out, including a very daring little change of key for the last verse, and we were in full song when Emile yet again rapped suddenly on his music stand and the musicians stopped playing. I looked around to discover the cause and saw a distinguished posse of gentlemen being ushered deferentially into the studio. Emile whispered that it was 'Monsieur Pierlot, le Premier Ministre', just flown in from London where he had been with the Belgian Government in exile. He had come to record an address to the Belgian people. So we slipped away to a waiting room.

While awaiting our return to the recording studio I got into conversation with a white haired musician. He must have heard my name, for he shook my hand warmly and announced that he was Albert Sykes whose father, a Tommy in the First World War, had come from Yorkshire, married and settled in Belgium. His Dad must soon have died or left home, for Albert spoke no English. He proudly presented me with a sheet of printed music, indicating a caption at the foot which read:

> Hymne Officiel de l'URSS trasncrit de la
> Radio Moscou et Imprimé durant l'occupation
> Allemand en Belgique
> par
> A. SYKES
> Vendu au Profit des Musiciens Tuberculeux.
> Prix 20 Francs.

I cannot read music so I have never known the qualities of this official hymn; presumably it is the music one hears rather too frequently at the Olympics.

Eventually we were allowed back to the recording room and a satisfactory version was accepted. I was promised all kinds of fame and fortune when the record was issued – and I then bolted back to Army HQ.

Next I went to Canadian Army HQ and, with the jeep's clutch on the way out, I nevertheless started on my V1 site recce with a look at a site near Crécy among others, and later drove on to Hesdin. There were air photographs of some of the sites and some were known to have been operational. The site at Hesdin had 'ramp still up'.

I had acquired a map of the area west and north of Amiens, and I marked a great number of red spots, representing suspected V1 sites, with black spots indicating the much fewer but more ominous and less understood V2 sites.

My object was to examine a cross section of red sites, studying the type and efficiency of camouflage measures taken. There were presumably hundreds more sites stretching back across Belgium, Holland and into Germany, and such a ground study of the characteristics and typical concealment of French sites would help the air photo interpreters to recognise these others. Since no one had given me any accurate information about the V1 weapon itself, I was unprepared for what I would see and I had to deduce the nature and operation of the weapons. The site I visited and photographed had been elaborately concealed or disguised, but had nevertheless been very comprehensively blitzed by the Allies. Others had either never become operational or had been dismantled by the retreating Germans. Locals were full of dramatic stories, including delighted reports of 'accidental explosions' and lots of dead Boches.

Gradually I was able to piece together the modus operandi of the V1. Essentially there was a metal ramp pointing up at a low angle, normally on a compass bearing for London. There were concrete store rooms, sometimes disguised as farm buildings by painted details of windows, etc. I never saw an actual bomb; more

Reconnaissance of V1 and V2 sites December 1944

Damaged ramp

'Dumb Bells'

accurately this was a small flying machine which carried the explosive over the target area and then the motor cut out causing the plane to glide down and detonate.

In some sites there were quantities of huge metal dumb-bell like objects. Where a ramp was still standing one could see that it consisted of a metal tube with a narrow slit opening, running the length of its top. Since the dumb-bells had a corresponding 'snib' projection it was not difficult to deduce that they were fired up the tube, like a shell up a gun barrel, and that the V1 plane was hitched to the snib. When launched violently at great speed the plane's rocket motor started up and carried it off, the 'dumb-bell' dropping off almost at once. In one field directly in front of the launch ramp there were dozens of the metal projectiles lying unrecovered.

Having made my report (with photographs) of these V1 sites my next posting, on 15 September, was to the 3rd Canadian Division. This Division had landed on the centre of the British Zone (Juno) between the 50th British Div on their right flank (Gold) and the 3rd Div on their left (Sword). I had no personal contact with them at the time of the landings, but had heard that some Regiments had a reputation for very tough behaviour towards the Germans – notably prisoners.

I received the same warm and unquestioning welcome as I remembered from the New Zealand and South African Forces in the Western Desert. At the time I joined them their task was to invest Calais, where the retreating Germans had left a garrison manning the very strong and elaborate defences, as they had also done in Boulogne and at the large calibre cross-Channel battery and lighthouse at Cap Gris Nez.

There were clearly no real camouflage needs either in concealment or deception, and I was directed to help the Chemical Warfare Officer. His task was a delightfully direct and relatively simple one. It arose from the fact that the Divisional concentration around Calais, and the preparations for the artillery barrage, were partly observable from the lighthouse at Cap Gris Nez, and fire from the heavy guns there could be brought down on both troops and guns from, as it were, behind their backs.

Constant efforts were made to topple the lighthouse by shelling and bombing (as, indeed, had the German guns across the Orne on the Ouistreham lighthouse – also a very effective observation post). All had been unsuccessful.

The heavy Cap Gris Nez guns (about 16in calibre) used to open up unceremoniously on communication centres in the area. I was in Marquise when this happened, and because my attention was directed up the road leading north from Marquise to Wissant on the Channel coast, where we had to lay a smoke screen, I did not realise that I must have passed through Marquise more than four years before, in May 1940, during the wild flight from Boulogne to Calais in the uncontrollable Signals car.

We settled into a German communication network junction box. This was a concrete building above ground and large enough for Bond, the CW Officer, his NCO, Heath, Fitzsimmons and myself, to take up residence. It lay to the west of the Marquise-Wissant road and only about 5,000 yards from the Cap Gris Nez strongpoint. There was no window or loophole in the building, only a heavy metal door. Snug as it was, I remember thinking as I was falling contentedly asleep that, if our smoke screen was achieving its object of frustrating the German garrison, they might send a sortie in strength to frustrate *us*. The Nazi garrison was reported to be Marines, and one assumed that Marines, German or otherwise, would be tough and enterprising.

The Cap Gris Nez position was very lightly 'invested'. I went up to the little village nearest to the perimeter and saw hardly a single Allied soldier. We had good prior notice of the main bombing effort against Cap Gris Nez, and I decided to go up to the vantage point of Bellevue, which was a captured German Radar station. I went up alone a short time before the raid was to start, taking with me an American carbine automatic which had a very fast rate of fire and made me feel relatively warlike.

Leaving the jeep on the near (east) side of the Bellevue hill, I walked up into the empty Radar station and looked round the deserted buildings. The Mess room contained RAF 'scalps' on the walls, propellers and bits of aircraft, and I looked for the best viewpoint overlooking the strongpoint. Below me, about 4,000 yards away, stood the lighthouse, and spread around below it was the cross-Channel battery and other clearly discernable defence installations. The place was well cratered from previous bombing, and there were some strange roughened grooves cutting straight across the crest of the Bellevue hill, in a direct line to the guns.

I focussed my binoculars on the gun turrets, which were in sunken pits and rotated with a camouflage 'lid' attached which moved round with the gun. As I looked the turrets all began to rotate, twisting away from the coast clockwise towards Bellevue. I realised, as in a bad dream, that if they kept turning I would shortly be looking directly down the barrels of these monsters, and at the same moment grasped the cause of the huge grooving on the hills – 16in shells fired point blank. As I watched, mesmerised, the sinister black mouth of the gun faced me momentarily and moved on. By now, the marker aircraft was overhead, a speck in a clear sky and flak had opened up from the defences, while a long glittering line, a pointer, descended from the plane to the centre of the battery.

By now a deep resonant hum was throbbing the air and, searching about with the binoculars over the Channel, I picked up a dark smudge. This grew into a cloud made up of swarms of Allied bombers, and the sound swelled to a stupefying roar, punctuated by detonations which puzzled me as no bombs had yet been dropped. When I looked back at the German guns I was astonished and impressed to see that they were trained on some inland target and calmly carrying out their regulation barrage.

The scene was both exciting and horrifying. I was about to witness some 1,000 heavy bombers, all intent on obliterating a few acres, and as I had my camera and a roll of film I was determined to record it all. Sticks of bombs began to burst across the position, and through the binoculars I hoped to see a direct hit – but soon dust

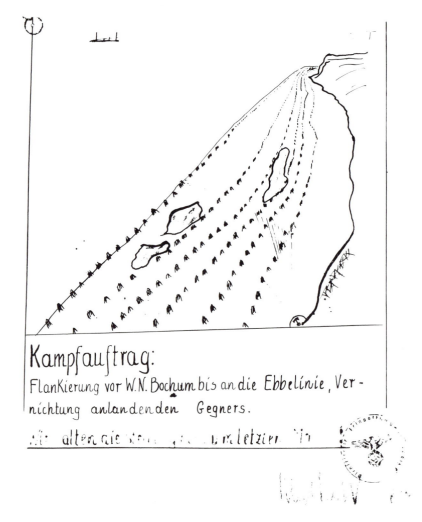

Kampfauftrag:

Flankierung vor W.N. Bochum bis an die Ebbelinie, Ver-
nichtung anlandenden Gegners.

.:· alten aie ·.·... ..· ι. ιι.l etzιeι ·'ιι

and smoke oblitered any clear view of the targets. At this moment, as in a realistic war film a flaming bomber crashed into the dust over the battery area.

The impact of sound – bursting bombs, Ack-Ack and the roar of aircraft – was beginning to freeze me where I lay, bringing a feeling of extreme isolation. Then a stick of bombs straddled the open fields at the very foot of Bellevue, about halfway between me and the target. I realised then how foolhardy I was, and scurried into a deep trench which was part of the system of intercommunications –

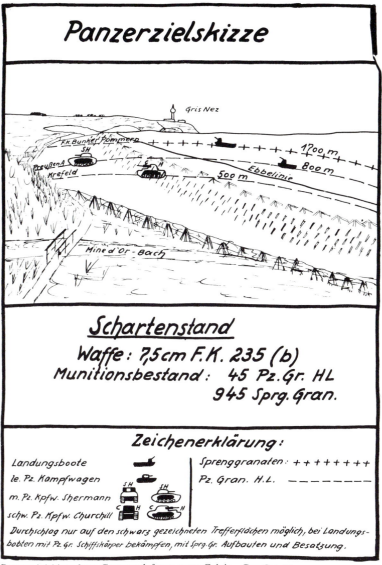

Panzerzielskizze from German defence posts Calais – Cap Gris Nez area

197

but from there I could see nothing of the bombing and its effect.

Feeling unnerved, solitary and still very vulnerable, I saw the trench entered a tunnel and hurried into the depth of this sanctuary, lurching deeper into the darkness and seeing nothing at first – but stumbling over an obstruction on the floor of the gallery. I stopped and, my eyes becoming accustomed to the darkness, I saw that the object on the ground was a crumpled figure with a German steel helmet.

My expedition had now turned completely sour, but I did not dare move back into the open or deeper into the tunnel. I just stood in the sheltering darkness until, eventually, the thundering tailed off and only the crumps of individual sticks of bombs could be heard. When all was quiet I picked my way out, past the German corpse which now I could see quite clearly – but kept my eyes away from the details of this dead enemy.

When Heath and I visited the captured coastal positions around Escalles, the booty consisted of a set of well designed German eating irons (cutlery), a very nicely produced and illustrated guidebook to France for Germans, also the Panzerweilskizze of some of the very formidable gun positions commanding the beaches near Cap Blanc Nez – very near the Sangatte (French) battery position which fired at the *Ben Lawers* as she left Calais in May 1940. Strangely, I cannot remember seeing the English coast which must have been clearly visible from this high cliff in reasonable weather.

I was looking forward to revisiting Calais and seeing again the places from which I had been so lucky to escape. The defence overprint showed that the Old Town, including the Rue de Moscou and all the little restaurants, had been demolished. I saw again the house on the corner of Rue des Quatre Coins, and the doctor's house where I had been billeted before the final panic set in. The Gare Maritime buildings still stood, as did the locks and basins where the ferry had berthed. I had a warm feeling of thankfulness that the evil of the evacuation had now been expunged.

On a different scale are my memories of good hauls of mushrooms in the dewy fields and of fruitful egg bargaining. Mollison, an English Intelligence Officer attached to the Canadians who spoke Dutch, taught me some useful phonetic phrases, such as 'Ma Frau, kan ick van u een paar eiren keunnen copen?' which I understood to mean 'Madam, can I buy from you a few eggs?' It seemed to work well.

The period from 3 October to 9 November was a restless time with a succession of HQ moves from Knesselaere, near Bruges, towards Eecloo, near Ghent, ten miles east, and finally to the south side of the Leopold Canal. These were all soggy tented camps, with HQ offices in command vehicles which were warmer and more comfortable than the tents. One lucky young HQ officer had acquired an airman's electrically heated overall suit and also fur lined boots.

The operation which the 3 Canadian Division undertook after Calais was the clearing of an area lying to the south of the entrance to the Schelde, opposite Walcheren Island. There was urgent need for the Allies to take Antwerp, get the docks into action, and thus enable the advance into Germany to be pressed forward. To thwart this, the Germans had again left delaying garrisons. The flooded and impassable land favoured defence, and the Leopold Canal turned the area virtually into an island. A small and costly bridgehead was pushed beyond the Canal quite near the 3 Canadian Div's latest HQ, but progress beyond was halted.

I flew over the 'island' in a slow Auster reconnaissance plane and only then appreciated the state of the country below. Eventually a sea assault was made from the Schelde estuary, and the whole area was cleared, including Walcheren – and the Schelde was open for ships to go through to Antwerp. Effective camouflage was at a discount, although I did produce a paper on concealment which was well received.

On 3 October my diary reports, 'Very wet. New recce with Earl, Home via Bruges in moonlight.' I had been asleep in the open back of a truck and awoke in the square at Bruges. It was like wakening into a dream world, to open one's eyes to the fantastic skyline of the richly varied medieval and Baroque towers and turrets standing out black and sharp against the moonlight.

12 October, 'Very slack day. Paint in afternoon in Earl's hut. To Ghent. Lovely hot bath. First real one since 17 May (Chichester).' Reading between the lines hot baths and mushrooms seem to loom large in the routine of these days.

The next move was to Termonde, to another training job, which filled me with dismay. Termonde was a typical tidy little Flemish town with canal and bridges, about halfway between Ghent and Brussels. I reported to training HQ which was situated on the outskirts, one of a number of large Victorian-type houses standing back from the road behind impressive gateways. When, days later, I returned with Heath and Fitzsimmons in our jeep and trailer for yet another attachment, we drove out over the bridge and along the road as before. However, when we had gone well beyond the outskirts and still had not seen the HQ, we turned and drove back, looking more carefully, and came to an elaborate gateway with a drive leading to a heap of rubble. Apparently, a day or so earlier, a V2 bomb had landed on the building, killing all 14 occupants. We had to search Termonde for another British Army office to which we could report.

At first we were billeted in a gaunt Belgian barracks which had been occupied by the Germans, and we were shown a high-walled yard where hostages and captured resistance men had been executed. Happily we were soon billeted with some people in the town. I had a very clean and comfortable (if cold) room in the house of a family named Van der Voorde. The father was a white haired man of advanced years and immaculate appearance, who spoke beautiful English. When I asked him where he had learned to speak so fluently he replied, 'At school, of course.' Fitzsimmons was billeted there as well. Madame and Mademoiselle Van der Voorde fussed over us – and Mademoiselle's financé kept an eye on the situation.

I was supposed to train 38 and 39 RHU which, if my interpretation is correct, meant Reinforcement Holding Unit. I cannot remember what my lectures were about, and was delighted when this particular attachement came to an end.

13

During the period 12-21 November my camouflage work, at this stage of the war, was concerned with the air defences of Antwerp. The Camouflage Pool Officers came together to work on this, and I saw a lot of Basil Spence, Tom Rose, Maurice Green, and others, and we managed between us quite a lively social life in the evenings. The US AAA (Anti Air Attack) HQ and 15 AAA Battalion, were deployed to the east of Antwerp to intercept bombers and reconnaissance, also V1 flights aimed at the vital Antwerp Dock area, but they were insufficient to put up a continuous screen. It was important, therefore, to conceal the real sites so that the Luftwaffe could not exploit the gaps.

It was quite strange and refreshing to be working with US troops. The first Lieutenant I worked with was a real soft-speaking southerner who looked like Gregory Peck, and he liked to philosophise at length. When I arrived at one site armed with my copy of Gen Armstrong's Order, the troops were all resting in their, to me, unfamiliar pyramidal tents. They were called out on the double. When told that the reason for the call was that they were to be instructed on good camouflage of their battery, one disgruntled GI exclaimed, 'Gee – camouflage against cock-sucking buzz bombs. Jesus Christ. Now I *have* seen everything!' The 27 November Thanksgiving Day meal, which I was invited to attend, was quite unexpectedly delicious – turkey and pumpkin pie and plenty to drink.

At the beginning of December I was involved in another aspect of the effort to misdirect the German attacks on Antwerp. The V2 weapon's details were still rather a mystery, but they were falling regularly in and around Antwerp. Heath and I had seen one land a few hundreds yards away across open farmland when visiting No 32 gun of the 789 Battalion US. When I say 'seen' I mean we were facing the direction in which the huge explosion took place. Of course we saw nothing of the falling rocket. There was an urgent request out at the time for all possible fragments of such rockets to be collected and passed over to Intelligence. In this case we were able to find a few twisted metal pieces, one of which looked like part of a fin. This undetectable approach of heavy explosive should, I suppose, have had a bad effect on our morale, but somehow I do not remember ever thinking that one would get me.

On 3 December I embarked on a new job concerned with V2 craters and had to visit a typical selection to take measurements of their dimensions and note their appearance. Then I had to devise ways of rapidly simulating craters where no craters existed, and concealing the real ones. In this way it was hoped that the enemy's intelligence of where his rockets were falling would be falsified so that if, in actual fact, they were falling short, he would be fooled into thinking they were over pitching – thus his adjustment of range would be completely wrong.

Bleach was used to burn out and lighten the simulated blast area and was very unpleasant to spread manually. Blowing up a barrel full of bleach seemed a rapid way to create the effect. It certainly would have been pleasanter for the operator. However, it made entirely the wrong pattern.

On 18 December the 21 Army Group Camouflage Pool Officers were all alerted once more. This time we were to work with Artillery units in concealing a large concentration of guns which were to put down a very heavy and extensive barrage in the Nijmegan area in support of a push by 30 Corps. The countryside was under deep snow and the concealment problems were therefore quite altered. Tracks were more than ever a give-away to

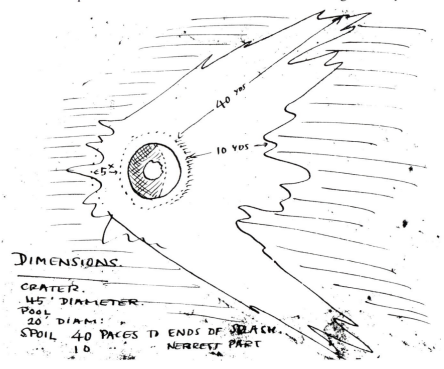

DIMENSIONS.

CRATER.
45' DIAMETER.
POOL
20' DIAM:
SPOIL 40 PACES TO ENDS OF SPLASH.
10 NEAREST PART

the air view, since it was possible at a glance to distinguish fresh tracks in current use. There was not much to be done about this, except to make use of as many non-military tracks as possible in so far as the tactical disposition of the guns would allow.

In place of green and brown toned nets a great deal of white calico was suddenly required. It was to the credit of the 21 Army Group stores planners that this was in fact available. The concealment work was going ahead and track-making being controlled where possible, when the German counter-attack through the Ardennes started (to be known as the Battle of the Bulge) and the British operation in the north was promptly suspended.

My movements on this operation had taken me across the German frontier at a point near Gennep in Holland. Like most long-awaited moments, it was something of an anticlimax. The jeep rumbled along a muddy track, and we would never have appreciated the great moment at all except for a notice, attached to a tree, which announced unceremoniously, **This is Germany. You have been warned.**

The Camouflage Pool were ordered to return to Army Group in Brussels, and here the atmosphere was very changed. Gone was the carefree euphoria, and one felt the very real fear of a German return that the Belgian people were trying to conceal. In some of the villages of the 'Bulge', to which the counter-attack had penetrated, the civilians who had welcomed the Allied liberators were harshly treated by the Nazis during their short return.

It was a strange time. A number of Camouflage Officers were billeted in a house vacated by a Rexist – 18 Rue Philomene in Brussels. This man, a member of the Belgian Fascist Movement, had fled with the Germans and had left considerable evidence of his sympathies. I kept a contemporary pamphlet of the 1938 elections, and we helped ourselves to the few remaining bottles of wine in his cellar, including a very good Figeac Cru St Emilion 1937. I also liberated a Rexist blanket, with a rather unpleasant modernist pattern, which is in use to this day.

I was still working on the V2 weapon crater project and had planned an observation flight, but at the time of Von Rundstedt's tank thrust the weather had closed down and day after day the Allied Air Forces were unable to get at them.

Christmas Eve. My diary reports, 'Weather cold, dry and clearer. Battle better.' This heralded some lifting of the gloom, so Basil Spence and I celebrated New Year's Eve at the Palace Hotel. Basil had disappeared to pay a visit to the gents just before midnight and was still away when the hour struck. Lights went out and pandemonium ruled for several minutes, with much kissing of strangers. When Basil reappeared he had a rather shocked and sheepish look, and I asked him what had happened. It seems that he had just started to pee when the lights went out and he was suddenly clasped firmly from behind, swung round and kissed several times about the face. When the lights returned he found himself staring into the ecstatic face of the large lady lavatory attendant!

I tried unsuccessfully to find out from the Decca people if my record was on the market, and then one evening Fitzsimmons announced that he had been to a variety show and the record had been played during the interval. As I was unable to contact Emile Deltour or Decca during the week, I decided to buy one. I did not know whether to be sorry or encouraged when the sales girl said they were sold out. The 1944 diary ends with a note: 'War 1,939 days. Overseas 1,406. D + 209.'

The snow returned on 8 January and on the 10th, when things were slack and we were still under thick snow, I was able to paint and go to a concert with John Hutton, also to see the *Henry V* Olivier film. And on 15 January I finally tackled the record people, who offered me a choice of 1½ per cent or 1,000 francs. I cannot remember what sort of temptation 1,000 Belgian francs would have represented in 1945, but I obviously had some confidence in my musical career for I chose the 1½ per cent royalties rather than an outright payment.

This is Germany. You have been warned

Reichwald January 1945

The 6 Airborne had returned to stiffen the resistance to the German push, but this was petering out and they were not seriously engaged. I renewed acquaintances and saw a little of the activity.

On 22 January the huge Artillery preparations in the area south of Nijmegan were once more set in motion (Operation Veritable, which had been interrupted by the Battle of the Bulge just before Christmas). Then a few days later my driver Fitzsimmons went on leave (Heath having already been granted leave) which was awkward, for I had to move about continually between various Artillery units, advising, controlling and organising the concealment of their gun positions and ammunition dumps. I was not feeling fit and was very exhausted. There were snow conditions and it was intensely cold until 30 January when a sudden thaw set in and made nonsense of the white camouflage. On 3 February some units still had their white nets over the gun positions.

Life was a strange mixture of comparatively comfortable and entertaining conditions in Brussels, and the opposite in the north east near Nijmegan, where the operation was being staged. Here the houses were all badly damaged and I was unable to find a building with either door or windows. A tent would have been preferable, but without Heath or Fitzsimmons, pitching a tent alone in deep snow and frozen ground was something to avoid. So I camped in odd shattered houses. What made the nights worse was the fact that I had contracted some skin infection which made me

205

Reichwald December 1944

Roof of 21 Army GP Brussels February 1945. Snow

itch violently and feel hot and feverish in the frigid conditions, so that I was forced to emerge from my bed roll and cool off, particularly my legs. I would then start shivering violently with the cold.

I went to a Canadian Field Dressing Station and was given a note to take to a hospital in the nearby town. Here I was allowed to take a steaming hot bath, laced with some very powerful germicide which burned my skin. My clothes and bedding had to be fumigated, but I emerged a new man. In the table of notable wartime baths this one ranks close to that one in Scotland after the D Day rehearsal. Apparently I had contracted scabies.

Back in Brussels on 8 February I managed to buy a copy of *Lilli Marlene*, and was told that 817 records had been sold. I received 580 francs.

All the Pool Officers were precedeing me on leave – Basil Spence on 11 Febraury, Tom Rose on the 13th, and Wally Cole, the ceramist, on the 15th. I decided that the names must have been taken out of a hat, for I had certainly served overseas longer (four years) than any of them.

During what proved to be the last few days of my 1,466 days of overseas service I was again up into Germany. The operation was in the Cleve-Goch corner of the Reich. The Canadians with whom I was working were in the Reichwald, a large forested area, and while I was wandering down a clearing I saw a movement among the trees ahead. I stood still and into view loped a huge fox. He approached to within a few yards and then suddenly, alerted by some scent or sound, he halted and looked me straight in the eyes; for what seemed a long time we regarded one another, then slowly and with great dignity, he turned aside and was gone.

Cleve, where Anne, Henry VIII's fourth wife hailed from, looked as if it had been a pleasant medieval town, but it was badly knocked about. I saw my first group of surly German civilians, and remembered the sign – 'This is Germany. You have been warned.' Any instincts of warmth towards people in distress had to be suppressed, and the time of rapturous welcomes was definitely over.

As I left, to return to Brussels on the way to my leave (which had at last come) another good healthy blow at the Fatherland was in progress, coded Blockbuster. I photographed a heavy gun in full recoil – quite a difficult moment to capture. The next evening I left Brussels and passed through Calais in the dark. No skulking in the cellars of the Gare Maritime this time, and no smell of singed flesh, or shelling from Sangatte.

Before the ship sailed at 0303 I stood at the rail and peered into the dimly recognisable features. Thank God, the nightmare of May 1940 was now history.

14

Jean and I celebrated our reunion at the Adelphi Hotel in Liverpool. I still have the bill – Capt and Mrs Sykes, Room 308. Bed and breakfast £1.16.0d. Service 4s. Then we took the train to Formby, where my father met us and took us to Jean's house, where her mother and Simon were waiting. My mother was ill in bed, following an attack during the previous week – I did not realise at the time that this attack had been a stroke.

Four days later we returned to London, where we stayed at the Euston Hotel. Kettners, where we had planned to have dinner was full, so we dined nearby, but Jean was unwell and was not hungry. I myself joined in the next day, and we both had a very bad night. Our reunion, yet again, was brief and blighted by ill health. I ended at the Casualty Receiving Station in Pembridge Gardens, in the care of a very cheery Irish doctor who assured me I'd be back on my feet in no time at all – at all.

I was moved to the ballroom, which had a flat roof composed of large panes of glass. There was a fairly regular thud of V1s or V2s landing somewhere in London, and the glass rattled violently each time. In the Ballroom ward I was alongside another officer whose ATS girlfriend stayed indefinitely whispering sweet nothings (1.30-8 pm), and it was exhausting lying, head averted, on one side. The next day I had my own visitor. Jean had been recovering at the Euston Hotel, and she called again on 12 March before leaving for Liverpool. It was at this time that news of the Rhine Crossing came through. I spent three more days at the Pembridge CRS, feeling low and without any energy, while the Irish MO cheerfully assured me he would get my temperature down and arrange for me to have extra leave.

On 16 March I was discharged and caught the first possible train to Liverpool, where my father, Jean and Simon met me. My father, suspicious of a sinister cause for my lack of fitness, arranged for me to see one of his Liverpool specialist colleagues and for my chest to be X-rayed. Later I remember Jean dancing with glee and waving a piece of paper – the medical report, showing that I had a patch on the lung. This would mean, Jean declared, hospitalisation and a prolonged stay in England.

I was sent to a Military Hospital near Chester, where I stayed for a fortnight. Jean visited me, bringing Simon and her mother, and we walked round Chester's ancient walls. Finally, on 13 April, Jean and I set off for London again, for I was anxious to have my war drawings submitted to the Committee of the War Artists Council. This time we stayed at the Royal Court Hotel in Sloane Square and shopped in the King's Road, buying, among other things, a strange old American Bagatelle board game called 'Nesting Birds'. This was much loved and used – but eventually the springs gave out.

We returned to Formby and spent our time between Jean's house and the family home in Formby. We made a couple of pre-war type car trips to North Wales and the Trough of Bowland – then, on 26 April, my leave was over. I reported to the Royal Engineers Depot – no longer at Chatham but now moved to Halifax – where I had another X-ray and Medical Board examination. Then began an endless and dreary period of waiting for a new posting. I tried, without succeses, to get help from Barkas and Robb at the War Office, but after absence from the 21 Army Group Pool my connection was broken and I reverted to RE Base automatically. I had to report to the RE Headquarters each morning, but as no posting came I worked on paintings of remembered episodes of the war. I was also called to sit on Courts Martial, of which there was a steady stream – mostly of troops who had gone AWOL (absent without leave) or failed to report on overseas postings. On 2 May my diary entry reads: 'Papers report Hitler dead.'

VE Day in Halifax was a real let down. The current court martial was, at least, called off, but when some celebrating troops started singing at the Old Cock Inn they were forced – on this day of all days – to stop as the place had no licence for musical entertainment! A curious people, the British – defiant in defeat, miserable in victory, or so it seemed.

On 16 May the Medical Board passed me A1 and at the end of the month, having been given 48 hours leave, I went to London and unsuccessfully pestered the War Office for a posting. I had left my prized D Day sniper's rifle at 21 Army Group, and from the War Office I telephoned the Army Group people who I was assured would have it. An officious Major asked me for all details of my booty – then announced that he ought to have me court martialled for disobeying Army regulations about captured weapons. No doubt he had confiscated it for himself. So that was the end of my sniper's rifle and, indeed, of all the other little souvenirs I had collected and left behind in Belgium when I came on leave.

A posting at last came through – to the ISTD (Interservices Topographical Department), which was housed in Mansfield (Theological College) in Oxford. The kind of topography I was to be concerned with was a new departure, aiming to supply information about available cover for concealment within the mapped area, and I spent a lot of time poring over stereoscopic photographs identifying types of vegetation. The mapping was naturally concerned with the Far East – the European war being over. It would have served me well had I been posted to the Far East, for I was able to confer with Far East experts who had first hand experience of what cover could be expected from the characteristic vegetation. I was concerned with the Singapore area and was able to study in great detail the air view of the route the Japanese had taken when they captured Singapore.

I was billeted in a hotel for a day or two and then found digs in St John's Street, but I was still travelling around with my camp kit and bed roll. I finally became aware that I was now to enjoy a strictly non-operational life, living comfortably in houses and following a near peacetime lifestyle. Most of the people working at the ISTD seemed to have been there throughout the war and the atmosphere of Oxford in June was calm and beguiling. I played in a cricket match – 'Over Thirties versus Under Thirties' – and realised, with a jolt, that I was now in the first category. I rowed on the river and swam, and I attended a life drawing class at the Technical College. Also I spent time looking at the treasures in the Bodleian Library and the Ashmolean Museum.

Digs or billets were a constant problem. My first room in St John's Street had a very strange landlady. She seemed reasonable at first – told me T. E. Lawrence had lodged there and recounted how superstitious he had been. Then I made the mistake of leaving some life drawings, not by any means lying about, but her prying eyes found them. That was the end of my residence. I believe her utter disapproval of artists stemmed from experiences with students from the Slade School (evacuated to Oxford earlier in the war).

My dismissal came promptly, but without the drama she obviously anticipated. It happened that I had been in some difficulty with Army pay since my arrival in Oxford, and that day I had hurried back to my digs to see if a postal order had come. It had, and with haste I would be just in time to cash it before the Post Office closed. But Mrs Boswell, the landlady, stood in the approved landlady's stance, arms akimbo, and barred my exit.

'I'll have to ask you to leave' she said sternly. I nodded and tried to make my escape. 'Don't you want to know why?' she asked, and added after a pause, 'It's because one of my regulars is coming back, you see.'

I said I was sorry and tried to slip out.

'Don't you want to know the real reason?' she persisted.

All right – some time later' I replied.

'It's you being an artist' she announced, with a cold look of condemnation, and she was about to enlarge on her reasons for the real reason. But I could wait no longer.

'Actually I'm a soldier' I replied, and bolted for the Post Office.

In July David Jeffreys came and stayed a couple of days, and Jean came later. VJ Day came at last, and I went to London for the day, standing among the masses of people outside Buckingham Palace and waiting for King George VI and the Royal Family to appear on the balcony. It was a very different scene from the depressing VE Day celebrations in Halifax.

All endeavour at ISTD was now more academic and unreal than ever, there being no call for maps of the Far East or any other theatre of operations. Looking back I find it hard to believe that I had another long 27 weeks until my demobilisation. Some events helped to keep the boredom and frustration at bay. Johnny Codner (whose tent in the desert I inherited, decorated with the nude lady) was posted to join me. He arrived a week after VJ Day and his wit and appreciation of the silly side of our situation made it all bearable, and even memorable at times.

Another helpful element was the discovery of a wealth of mushrooms right in the heart of Oxford. While taking a lunch break stroll in the meadows I came upon a haul such as I had not seen even in the best parts of Belgium and Holland. Each lunchtime Johnny and I used to slip quietly in and out on our mushroom haunt, carefully secreting our haul.

One highlight of this time was a return visit to Belgium. Either Johnny or I had the idea of doing a test run of the usefulness and feasibility of the ISTD 'cover map' idea, and we procured the necessary air photographs of Belgium from the Air Photo Interpretation HQ at Medmenham, on the Thames. The choice of Belgium for this exercise was not unconnected with memories of the warmth and kindness I had experienced there and the number of friends I had made.

Having completed our cover maps we asked for arrangements to be made to fly us to Brussels, and were duly authorised to fly from Croydon. On arrival we were loaned a vehicle and dutifully checked out the terrain, making notes of the accuracy of findings.

The area of Waterloo fell within the zone of our recce, and we were able to visit the Museum on the mound, which conveyed the battle very vividly. I met some of my Brussels friends, obtained royalties from Decca together with some copies of the record for my family, and we were back in Oxford on 21 October.

Johnny was demobilised three days later, but two more old comrades reappeared – John Baker and Robert Medley, and we indulged in lengthy reminiscences of what was by now becoming the golden period of our war – the Western Desert.

I joined a carpentry class run by the Army Education people, for Simon had expressed a wish for a dolls' house, and the one I designed and made was more or less in the Georgian style, with elaborate double-curved steps leading to the grandiose front door. Christmas leave enabled me to spend Christmas Day at Formby once more. It was very like old times, but my father was not on form and my mother also was much changed. My brother, John, was there and we went through the dressing-up ritual, but missing from the dressing-up cupboard, alas, was my father's 1914-18 topee.

I took the dolls house home, determined that Simon was going to enjoy it. I must still have been a very unsympathetic dad, full of unreasonable expectations of what Simon would, or should, enjoy. He had no child friends and seemed to be surrounded only by doting adults (my father, Jean's mother, and so on), so I invited some other children round to help him enjoy the dolls' house – which, after all, he had said he wanted. It was placed in the garden, and I myself took some part in the game – meaning to leave the children to it when they had become involved. Presently I realised that Simon was not with us. He had retired to the house and locked himself in, and it was some hours before he could be persuaded to open the door. Later he developed an acute 'poison phobia', which made life very difficult, and it was decided that he was psychologically disturbed by my return home. In some ways it was a relief to be back in Oxford.

On 20 February 1946, my war service ended. I once more visited the RE Depot in Halifax, and was sent to a grim looking woollen mill used for the issue of demob suits. I handed in my pistol, compass and other odds and ends. Then I walked out into Civvy Street.

Wartime correspondence

TO:- MAJOR S.B.SYKES
R.E.
C.T.C
M.E.F.

29 November 1943.
Greetings from Jean

Cross out anything below which does not apply. Do not write anything on this side of the card except the date and your signature. If you write anything more than that, the card will be destroyed.

(Postage must be prepaid on any letter or post card addressed to the sender of this card)

I am quite well.

~~I have been admitted into hospital.~~

{ sick } and am going on well.
{ wounded } and hope to be out again soon.

~~I am being sent down to the base.~~

~~I have received your~~ { letter(s) dated............
{ telegram ,, ...
{ parcel ,, ...

I will send you a letter as soon as possible.

I have received no letter from you.
{ lately.
{ ~~for a long time.~~

SIGNATURE
ONLY } Steven to Sykes. cgt.

Date....9..Jun.44.....

28 4 44 G.H.Q.P.P. 3,290M.

213

EPILOGUE

After the war I sometimes felt drawn to revisit the Middle East and, in Egypt and Libya, experience again the magic of the Western Desert, which had planted a strong nostalgia in many who served there. Very few had before, or have since, existed so close to nature free of urban life and, in my case, come so near to having a hand in the momentous events of the war. However, such a return would have proved a lonely pilgrimage without any of my Eighth Army comrades.

In 1962 I went on holiday in France with my two younger children, Nicholas and Clare, born in the years just after the war. At Calais, before disembarking, I looked again at the Gare Maritime and the area around the port, still laid bare by the defensive demolitions of the Germans. I felt a sudden impulse to shout at the milling, impatient tourists, 'Don't you realise what happened here?'

We drove to the area of the Normandy landing, stopping briefly in Beuzeville. I had brought my large Normandy scrapbook, containing pictures taken just after the liberation. One, of L'Auberge Cochon d'Or, which in my photo of 1944 had just ceased to be the Nazi Kommandantur, shows Nicholas holding the scrapbook; he takes the place of an excited local wearing some kind of cuirassier's or fireman's casque in the earlier picture. Gone were the crowds and resistance fighters with strange antiquated firearms slung on their shoulders.

While having drinks in the little garden in front of the Cochon d'Or, I opened the album at the Beuzeville page and invited the waitress to look at it. At first she was puzzled and looked at me enquiringly – and then the franc dropped. The rest of the staff were excitedly called out to look. Next the photo of the jeep standing in the main street was scrutinised and everyone trooped off to show it to the present shopkeepers. The shops, although much changed, are easily recognisable by the architectural features, arches and balconies. Changes of ownership are evident. The florist's shop of Monsieur F. Levieils in 1944 belonged to Monsieur Clause in 1962 and to J. P. Gatinet in 1984. Next door the Quincaillerie of 1962 has become Pomme d'or, selling fromage, and so on. How short and mutable are men's endeavours!

Beuzeville Epilogue P.1.

23 August 1944 Liberation

Revisit 1962. Same shops, new trades

3rd visit 1984. Still the same shops and again new trades

Liberation 23 August 1944 before the ex Kommandantur

1962 Revisit with children Nicholas and Clare

1984 Revisit for *Sunday Times* article 40th Anniversary D Day

It was confusing to rediscover the small roads down to the landing beaches, and I caused outraged consternation among the local traffic by driving around on the left of the road – so preoccupied was I with locating the haunts of 6 June 1944. Nicholas shared my disapproval of what had been done to the 0880 Strongpoint, cleared of most of the Atlantic Wall works and peppered over with ugly beach bungalows. However, the two tall villas remained and other familiar features were pill boxes in the new back gardens.

Early in 1984 an increasing interest in the approaching fortieth anniversary of D Day became evident. I still had the photographs I had taken with my old bellows camera (a Voigtlander) on landing on Queen White at H (hour) + 195 on 6 June and subsequently, and having discovered that the official photographer for this sector had been wounded on landing, before he had recorded this operation, I offered my unpublished pictures to the *Sunday Times*. The Editor of the Colour Magazine was enthusiastic. I also showed him my scrapbook containing photos, maps and briefing material, including air photos of the 0880 Strongpoint area of 6/7 June, and much else. The *Sunday Times* appointed a writer, and with him I revisited Normandy, later being joined by a French photographer.

We drove in a hired car from Cherbourg, passing the American beaches of Utah and Omaha, the 50th British Division and Third Canadian Division, and eventually reached the 3rd British Division area. With mounting excitement the familiar landmarks were recognised. I had relied on the water tower at the back of the 0880 Strongpoint, still standing in 1962, as a good marker – but it had gone. Otherwise the scene was much as it had been – the holiday villas and bungalows, mostly deserted and forlorn in the stormy April weather.

The two tall villas still stood and we found some of the pill boxes, much overgrown, in the gardens within the perimeter of the 0880 Strongpoint. This area was photographed to provide a present-day comparison with the D Day photos. To bring in a bit of action I was asked by the French photographer to leap over a tidal channel in the huge expanse of glistening sand left by the ebbing tide. Not quite seeing the point, I took the leap – and the resulting picture was more evocative of the old 'Skegness is so bracing' poster by John Hassall than anything that could have occurred on 6 June 1944 – but at least it proved that I could still jump!

Guided by the photos in *Captain Sykes' Portfolio* (as the *Sunday Times* article had dubbed the scrapbook) we decided to try to contact the kind couple who had welcomed Sgt Heath and me so warmly in Villers-sur-Mer on 23 August 1944. On our way eastward we passed through Beuzeville and again photographed the subjects taken in 1944 and 1962. In Villers-sur-Mer the album again proved effective in reawakening the past.

The lady in the Town Hall immediately recognised Monsieur and Madame Chorin but informed us that they had moved to Vire some 80 km away. Warned of our sudden visit by phone, we were once more warmly received and the album pored over.

I hope, when the 50th anniversary comes around, to celebrate it with a quiet and solitary visit to those D Day beaches, and that the two tall villas, the overgrown pill boxes, and the site of the 0880 Strongpoint, will still be there.

Mme Chorin, Steven Sykes, Sergeant Heath after liberation, Villers Sur Mer 23 August 1944

9 Rue d'Aigneau Vire 1984

La Breche the two tall villas 1984

'Normandy is so bracing'